The IT Girl

3 Steps to Find Career Options for Young Women in Tech

Sheekha Singh

The IT Girl © Copyright 2021 Sheekha Singh

For more information, email contact@sheekhasingh.com.

ISBN: 978-1-7775463-0-4

GET YOUR FREE GIFT!

Get to know more about me and be a recipient of my modern letter. Enroll here to be a part of the family. Link to subscribe: https://sheekhasingh.com/sheekha-singh/

To experience this book best, I invite you to schedule a **free** 20-minute consulting session with me personally, to implement the ideas faster and find resources to help you/your child/friend/relative/student in taking the next steps needed to find the right position in Tech.

Schedule your first free consultation
session by visiting my website.
Link to schedule:
https://sheekhasingh.com/sheekha-singh/

First 20 callers with a proof of paperback book get a **free** 'IT Girl' **T shirt**. Share your picture with the hashtag #theitgirl and tag me in your pictures on Instagram, Facebook and Twitter.

Email to know more details.

Dedication

To the woman who forced me into IT:

Look, Ma, I am a writer now!

&

To the man who always played the devil's advocate:

It worked, and sh*t is getting real now, husband!

Table of Contents:

Foreword

It is rare that you meet a person who is the voice of their generation. How do you recognize one, you may ask? Look for boldness, the inquisitive mind, explorative, adventurous nature, the passion, and empathy. You will never forget the encounter with someone like that.

Every year I organize an international annual conference for senior IT leaders and managers in New York. I was fortunate to welcome Sheekha as the speaker at the Test Leadership Congress. When I came across her proposal, I knew it was a message the attendees needed to hear. What happened next surprised me.

Usually, seasonal managers and industry veterans are hard to impress. People in the audience and on stage are peers; they know a lot and have been through a lot. Sheekha entered the stage as a representative of a younger generation- the millennials. Her topic was so important and relevant to everyone in the audience that literally nobody felt unaffected.

Sheekha's message stirred an emotional discussion in the audience. This topic forced us to think how we as managers can recognize and grow the talent of the younger generation. Discussions began around how to respect the differences and discover hidden inspirations and challenges that will shape the next generation's achievements.

The book you are about to read is Sheekha's journey. It is her story. It is a message for both the leaders and young people who aspire to succeed and excel in their technical career. Even more so, it is a message to young girls and women who seek a true role model. Sheekha is certainly one.

It is my pleasure to recommend this book. You will absolutely enjoy it as Sheekha is a talented writer. I urge you to read it and then, hand it to your daughter, your sister, or a young girl in your community. This book will most certainly make a difference to anyone who reads it.

Happy reading!

-Anna Royzman

Founder – Global Quality Leadership Institute and Test Masters Academy

Introduction

It was a warm summer day in Omaha. I could see the sunflowers swaying in my backyard. As I marveled at the beauty of nature, my phone dinged. I was excited because I received an email in my inbox with the subject line: Invitation to speak. I read the email and was thrilled. I was invited to speak at an international conference in Europe.

I threw my hands up in the air like that little white cute ghost emoji who looks like he is always positive and has a good vibe. If it could talk, it would say, "Yyayyyyy!!!"

I visited the conference website and glanced at the list of speakers. The first thing that I noticed was that no women were listed until I scrolled to page three. I saw one talk by a woman on page three and kept scrolling. The next talk by a female presenter that I found was on page five.

I was irked. I looked up at my phone and said, "Okay, Google, what's the number of women in technology right now?" What I saw on my phone changed me forever. I can never unsee that number.

My phone read: "Today, women make up only twenty percent of engineering graduates, and an even smaller number, sixteen percent, of the engineering workforce is made up of women. Google survey reported that many girls don't know what computer science actually means."

Girls do not know what computer science actually means!?! Is that for real?

I decided to ask my friends who grew up in the United States about this issue. I wanted to know why young girls don't choose careers in computer science. I heard one common answer. Girls in high school assume anything related to computers is tough. My friends also mentioned the lack of awareness of the different areas in this vast field.

I wanted to change this.

In the spur of the moment, I decided to communicate a message to all the girls out there. I want to help this generation of young women who have absolutely no clue about computer science. I wish to spread the word that technology is amazing, cool, lit, interesting, and not difficult.

I pictured myself standing on top of a stage and yelling the phrase, "IT is cool! We need more women here!!!"

Back in 2008, I had no idea about computer science engineering. I didn't know anything about what creates a computer science course. A few years later, I graduated with my bachelor's degree, moved to the United States of America, earned my Master's degree, found a job that I actually love, and wait for it—found a way to marry my passion to my profession. The book that you are reading now is the result of that path.

This book debunks myths and helps young women choose a career in IT. Everyone thinks IT is only about coding, which is not true. Through my research, I intend to help young girls, working women, and parents.

This book reduces the hours needed to research computer careers, and I will help you decide which role to aim for. After reading this book, you can decide which job suits you or your children the most.

I offer a three-step process to help you find the tech job you would love the most. Implementing this process will benefit you in many ways. You will find your strengths, map your skill to an existing position, and get lit!

You will also learn why there is a need for more women in technology. I've made your life easier by doing all the research for you, presenting you with a list of jobs that do not involve programming and their average salaries based on recent market data.

It was a happy hour on a Friday night, and I was hanging out with a few of my friends who work in IT. I ended up asking questions about women in tech. After our happy hour, I realized that there has never been enough awareness about tech in the past few years. Everybody tells you that tech is a great field to get into, but nobody points out the multiple options available for people who don't want to code.

Back then, even I did not know all the options present in the IT world. I was never told that it was okay *not* to know how to write software and still have a wonderful career in IT.

Nobody told me this when I was in high school, getting ready to apply for universities. When it came to jobs, people always spoke about the "IT guy" and software developers. Clearly, it was due to a lack of awareness. It felt wrong.

Tech is a vast field. Many departments contribute to the success of a software application. For example, you could be great at writing software, but if you cannot market the app, your exceptional coding skills will be good for nothing.

Who knew social media strategist or social media marketing would be actual jobs?

Imagine how this will change in the next fifteen years.

My husband asked me why I was writing this book for just girls. I showed him the horrific numbers of women working in IT. I strongly feel that every girl has the right to earn, earn *well*, and be independent.

My mother forced me to get into IT, but, at this point, I am glad she did. I realized the importance of money, career, growth, and stability.

I am not a developer, but I love my job. Even though it doesn't pay as much as some other tech jobs, I am happy with the way I have designed my life. Now, I know what I am good at and which field I excel in, and working is a joy.

It took me six years to figure it out. If someone had told me, "Hey, Sheekha. Did you know you can have a career in IT without being a developer?" I would never have felt weird about being forced to take up computer science during my bachelor's degree.

I changed my course, my path, and I like what I do now. I knew I enjoyed public speaking, so I worked towards it, and now I'm being invited to speak at international tech conferences. I love to write, and I found a way to do that too. I weave tech into my writing.

I don't want any other girl to turn 28 and spend six years of trial and error trying to figure out what she is good at. It is high time that women have job satisfaction as well as a great work-life balance. I hope this book will help someone find their talent and an ideal position that they would love. I hope that every girl reading this excels not only financially but also mentally and emotionally—living a well-balanced life.

So, what are you waiting for, Girl?

I welcome you to the not so boring world of computers.

Begin your quest to explore the various options available for you in the world of technology. I hope you get inspired to join the tech world. I want you to be a badass woman who not just works but excels in her IT job and, most importantly, loves it.

I promise you that you will walk away without any confusion. You will have learned the cool range of positions that fit you and your style in the tech industry.

Follow the three-steps, and trust me, you will find a way to your ideal position and become the IT Girl.

—Sheekha Singh

Your techie millennial coach/friend you never knew you needed.

Sheekha Singh

8

Section 1

Sheekha Singh

Chapter 1

I know life sucks, and I know it is hard to design one that does not. They say having a good job is an important factor, along with having a good partner and good health. Knowing the value of these elements helps you design your best life. I can help you with the job part, but before that, you will have to start with the basics. And you'll have to get to know me better.

Have you ever seen hashtags like #MenInIT or conferences designed around men working in IT? It sounds weird, right? So, women, why is that?

I have a goal. It might seem audacious. I no longer want to see the separation of men and women in IT.

I do not want to see special treatment for women in tech; I want to see equality rather than special treatment at conferences for just women in tech. I'll tell you why but before I begin, let me tell you how I ended up here.

Once upon a time, in 1992, I was born in a middle-class house in the southern city of India called Hyderabad. I can paint a sad picture of how I struggled and eventually reached where I am today, but that would be a lie.

My father died when I was six years old. Despite that, I had a very normal childhood, and I was good at studying. I was an A+ student in school. I received the all-rounder award, and I used to participate in a lot of competitions. The thing with being an all-rounder is that I never felt I belonged anywhere. I always had the urge to be a pro in one field, but I also wanted to try everything else.

Growing up, I used to tell everyone that I wanted to become a doctor. My mom told me very clearly from the beginning that she couldn't afford the fees for my medical college. I had no other option but to take up engineering. I loved biology, but I knew how hard my mom worked to feed my sister and me, so I went with the flow.

Have you wondered why there are so many Indians in the engineering and medical field? That is because our parents condition us to compete in every field and earn a lot of money. Yes, everything is a competition when you grow up in a country of 1.3 billion people.

The boomers in India struggled. So, they excelled at forcing their unfulfilled dreams onto their children. They made sure that we millennials followed their guidance no matter what. There is no discussion. It is always a decision. Thus, in an Indian household, eighty percent of the time, children are forced to take up either medicine or engineering after high school. Middle-class people like us, who do not have enough money for medical school, go with engineering because it is cheaper. Also, the return on investment is faster.

That's the first reason for you to get into engineering.

If you are reading this book, you are either a student confused about your major or a parent trying to figure out a course that would be beneficial for your child's career. You could also be a working professional in IT who wants to change her path.

I am here to help you sort out that problem and steer you in the right direction, helping you find exactly where you fit. I do not want you to blame your parents or someone else for enrolling you into IT. Instead, I want you to wed your passion to IT, make a living out of it, and design your life the optimal way.

I know how it feels when you do not have someone in your family to guide you or tell you what matters. I know the feeling of not having a mentor or a career counselor. I also know how it feels when you are good at something but cannot pursue it as a career because it doesn't pay well enough.

I want to be that person for you.

I will attempt to help you realize the benefit of choosing IT as your career option and help you understand IT is not about coding. Get clear on this, girls; tech is not rocket science. Tech jobs pay well, and you can find ways to pursue your passion within the field.

I want you to feel like I am the elder sister you never had. Flip to my cover and picture me talking to you in a room. I do not know if you will choose IT after reading this book, but if you do, I will be super happy to know that you had me all along and that I helped you decide. I hope you will be one of those few people who knew what they were doing when choosing their major.

The foremost reason why I did not want to join IT was because I felt it was for guys and that it would be boring. Nobody explained the benefits of joining IT or told me what I would get out of this degree after four years of study. I could not find any guidance on the branches, positions, options, and domains available in this field. I believed a tech career meant that I would start coding and be in front of a computer for the rest of my life.

I am 28 years old, and I have always envisioned my life to be a certain way. Everyone does that. I am here to help you find what you are good at, apply that in IT, and fall in love with what you do.

I will be honest. I have loved writing since I was young. People told me writers don't earn much. I loved speaking. Public speaking was not a career option back then. The only thing I was sure of was that I needed to earn enough money. So, engineering was a perfect fit for me. I was told that engineers earn a lot of money as soon as they graduate. I heard that big organizations come hunting down fresh graduates and offer a job. I was happy with that.

Being middle-class has its perks. There is a constant urge to upgrade our life and the never-ending pressure to stop struggling. The only solution that you see is money. You grow up wanting to earn money and to be able to afford everything that you always dreamed of.

I will help you learn how to overcome this pressure of earning enough money.

In my opinion, first, we need to know what IT is and figure out your strength. We will then find your niche and map your skill to a position in IT. We move on to find you a career path in IT, all while learning from people who have been there and done that. You will find testimonials from women currently in IT and were once in the same boat as yours.

Read on, and let us begin the journey.

****

Christina McGeorge, Solutions Consulting Lead (NCR) USA

What made you choose the Tech/Engineering field?

I love the sciences and problem solving. Coupled with that, I love interviewing and talking with customers to gain insight into the problems they face.

What career advice will you give to younger women out there?

Don't fall into the trap of over listening to those that outline reasons a problem cannot be solved and offer neither guidance nor encouragement associated with advancing solutions. Surround yourself with intelligent, positive individuals that foster your ability to think outside the box. Do this in your professional and personal life and you will see the world through a lens that will build your confidence and hone your skill set.

****

Avanija, Lead BioTechnologist, India

What made you choose the Tech/Engineering field?

Biotechnology! I've always been fascinated by biological science right from the school days. If there is one thought that popped up on my mind while choosing this field was "Would you enjoy doing this for the rest of your life?" The answer that echoed within was "Hell yes! Biosciences or nothing." To be able to answer the many Why's and the many How's what better way than understand how it works?

Well, my journey in this field was not an easy one. I had to face the toughest of times to get to where I am now. I cannot believe myself when I say that I landed a job during COVID. It required extreme patience & self-motivation (not-at-all-easy-to-do-this) but it surely did pay off. I'm working as a Lead Biotechnologist with an Indian Food Tech start-up Brew51 with a team of amazing women building some amazing stuff that'd change the way the world eats.

What career advice will you give to younger women out there?

The main reason for the small number of women in tech is due to the lack of role-models for women within the sector and this is mainly down to the gender stereotype of 'boys being better at science and math. To dissect the problem, we need to look at early development. At high school, girls achieve better grades than boys. Yet for females who do pursue computer science at university level, they find themselves being outnumbered by males.

A possible reason for why more girls don't pursue science related degrees is due to the 'pinkification' of girls in early age. Toys, clothes and job possibilities are still marketed towards gender despite recent developments in breaking this historic trend. It is time we focus on the next generation of tech talent, make sure gender equality exists for the good of everyone. This means more flexible working arrangements, more women in leadership roles & more encouragement at an early age for girls to pursue whatever they want.

I'd like to share some of the things I followed to get to where I am today.

- *Don't limit yourself to any one particular line of work. Be patient and focused.*

- *Know that you are worth much more than what you think you are. Give a deaf ear to those who try to demotivate you.*
- *Pursue it when they say it won't work & prove them wrong.*
- *Take risks. You'll have to sacrifice a lot of things but if you think it's only going to help you & others, just go for it.*
- *Don't be afraid of failures.*

Chapter 2

Why IT?

Upon Googling "why IT," you will find a hundred different reasons why to get into the field. All those reasons are solely based on careers that involve heavy coding.

Remember, I am not going to set unrealistic expectations. I am not saying that you will become the next female Mark Zuckerberg. I do not expect you to suddenly design the next greatest app in the market that will revolutionize the tech industry.

Nope. That is not happening. Although it would be amazing if it does. Instead, I'll guide you to do the exact opposite. Mark Zuckerberg knew what he was good at. We do not. Well, at least not at this stage.

We are here because we are confused, and we need direction. So, we are going to learn how not to be Mark Zuckerberg.

Not everyone becomes famous overnight. We all have to work, and I want you to know how to work and earn smarter.

I am here to help you find your answer to the question, "Why IT?"

After being in the field for almost seven years and learning from the brightest minds, I can vouch for these five reasons.

- Money
- Variety of Positions
- Creativity and Flexibility
- Career Growth
- Stability

Let's go into each of these in detail.

Money:

Let me be honest. If you hail from a middle-class background and do not want to be middle class, money will always be on your mind.

IT helps solve the money problem.

Technology is everywhere, and many people make a lot of money out of it.

Yes, you will be able to afford that Chanel bag and those Steve Maddens when you get into the tech world, Gal. Do you need any other reason?

On a serious note, the average salary for a computer science graduate is $75-80,000 in a decent city and a mid-size company. These are the numbers for positions that do not involve direct coding.

Once you have your degree and land a job, that is the least salary you would earn. This is the worst-case scenario. I mean, how bad can $75,000 be? If you stick with this field, you will only go higher from here.

Even if you get at least a two percent pay hike every year, it will be way more than you first expected. You will be able to afford Chanel, Michael Kors, and Steve Madden, all with a single month's salary.

To me, money was, and still is, the most important factor that will always stand out.

Let's talk about money and independence.

I love independent women. I like women who are strong and have powerful #bossbabe vibes. I like women who define themselves as strong, bold, and successful. Girls, if this is what you always wanted, then tech is for you.

You are bound to fall in love with the financial independence that you gain by working in any tech field. After paying your student loans, your salary will still allow you to save. I want that for you. I want this for all my readers. I want every girl on this planet to be independent.

I know it might sound cheesy but seriously, why should guys have all the fun? Think about it.

Why can't you be the Sugar Mama? Why can't you think of spoiling your partner by being able to afford the atrocious gifts? Why can't you dream of handling the house on your own and still be able to spend money on your hobbies? Why can't you go down on a knee and ask your partner with a diamond ring?

Why not?

When I asked my mom why she wanted me to get into tech, she always says it was for the salary. She realized that it took my sister and me two years to earn the money that took fifteen years of service for her.

That is the power of money in the technology world.

Think of that song by Arianna Grande, "I want it; I got it. I see it. I like it. I want it; I got it." Well, you will be able to sing that too if you join IT, Girls. You want it; you got it. No kidding.

Please do not judge me by Arianna's reference. I am more of a Cardi B gal. I don't really want a white horse and a carriage; I'm thinkin' more a white Porsches and carats—provided I buy those with my own money.

Ok, now back to harsh reality.

Emergency. Let us be honest. Our parents are aging as we age, and I, for one, do not like to ask others for even a dollar unless I am really broke. Some of us hate asking for money from friends and family. Do not get me wrong. It is okay to ask for help when you need it. I feel that when anyone in my family falls sick, I should be able to help them without the need to borrow money. Simply saying, I hate debt.

It took me four years to save enough and create a comfortable emergency fund. I owe that to the tech industry and STEM in general. My husband is not in the tech industry. Both of us can clearly make out the difference when it comes to savings, expenditure, and budget.

I have friends who have lavish habits, and if it were not for their IT salary, they would not have been able to afford their habits.

Variety of Positions:

Universities rarely do a great job explaining the breadth of IT positions available in the market. They just market an ideal software developer job, and for many girls, that is a big no. If I told you that your passion for drawing or painting is actually in high demand right now in the tech world, wouldn't you give a thought to choosing computers as your course of study?

There are many different courses and branches in computers other than programming and software development.

This, to me, was a huge relief when I bagged my first internship in India. In 2012, I helped create an animated logo for an android app that was version 4.0. I was super excited. I was like, oh my God! Animation deals with a set of images; it's not programming, and it is super fun! Who knew? Yay! I like it already. I was super thrilled to realize that I could get a tech job, get paid for not coding all day, and play with images.

Animation is one example, but many positions are creative and fun. I will cover that in detail in section three.

Creativity and Flexibility:

I am a firm believer that everyone on this planet is good at something. I added this point because, after seven years, I figured out where I fit. I know how to incorporate my talent into my profession.

I love Instagram. Instagram makes it seamless to upload, view, and scroll through thousands of images with a very simple design. Nothing is super complicated or hard when you use Instagram, and that is where creativity comes into the picture— creativity of the UI/UX department. By the way, User Interface (UI) and User Experience (UX) does not involve coding in any way.

When a person is a UX/UI designer, their main aim is to make the end-user feel comfortable when using a mobile or a desktop app. We need to be creative when figuring out how to display tons of data on a seven-inch screen.

Imagine designing an app for a car. Imagine designing an easy-to-use app for your grandmother so that she can log in to her bank account. Areas where creativity is needed to cater to the current and future generations is unlimited.

The demand for creativity increases as the screen size decreases. I would have never imagined that one day, I would be able to read my email on my watch while walking, running, or sipping coffee.

Go figure.

Flexibility:

It is a no-brainer that you need an internet connection to do anything on your phone other than setting an alarm. The tech world has plenty of options that help you work from anywhere in the world with just a laptop and an internet connection. That is it.

Digital nomads have become famous with good reason. Tech offers an opportunity to have a job that can be done remotely from anywhere irrespective of the time zone, and you have the flexibility of traveling the world and earning at the same time.

Hop onto Instagram and search for #digitalnomadlife, and you will be mesmerized. To achieve that, my girl, a tech job would be one of the best ways to create that lifestyle.

Irrespective of whether you want to travel and work, flexible jobs are great. I realized that during pandemics, tech jobs were some of the few that offered the flexibility of working from home, preventing a need to step outside your house.

Career Growth:

A common interview question is, where do you see yourself in the next five years? Yeah, I used to hate that question. If I had no clue where I would be in the next twelve months, how can I be sure where I see myself in the next five years? Right???

Thanks to my exposure in the tech field, and thanks to conferences that I attended, I was able to see exactly where and how I would like to see myself in the next five years. Exposure makes you see things that you never knew existed.

At my previous company, I had a Product Owner on my team. She would obtain the requirements from clients and transform them technically so that the engineers would be able to create and test those features.

I was very impressed by the way she spoke. We worked for a startup, yet she dressed impeccably. She carried herself well. She was also the chairman of the National ACH committee. After working with her, I realized what I wanted to look like five or ten years from now.

It is okay to go with the flow, but it is also important to have a goal and a vision in mind and to know what you want in life. I do not expect you to know at the age of 18 or 20. However, I would want you to visualize a goal and design your life around it. Only then will you be able to define success in your terms.

Success does not always equal money or fame. The definition differs from person to person.

There is no one size fits all. I want you to close your eyes right now and tell me how you wish to see yourself.

I always pictured myself in a business suit giving talks to 150 people. Although I have not achieved it, I did follow that vision of mine. I gave a talk in front of 80 people at a conference in a skirt and a blazer. That, to me, was a great f#&^ing deal. I call myself successful.

The whole point of this exercise was to make you believe in the opportunity for career growth in the tech world.

I am someone who requires proof. I am one of those who will look at the dentist's teeth before getting treated. So, hop on to Twitter, Instagram, or any other social media and see for yourself. You will be able to find mentors and inspirational women who have been there and done that.

Stability:

After a certain age, I have noticed that everyone craves stability in their life. I feel that perspective changes as you age. Although

I firmly believe in doing what you love, I feel what you're doing should be stable.

Moving out of my home country to the USA to study and work has taught me the importance of having a stable income.

Here are a few perks of having a stable income:

- You can afford a place of your own, even if it is a 500 square foot studio apartment. It is yours, and you can afford it with your own salary. You can start saving. I realized the importance of a stable savings account when my family members fell sick. I was happy because I could help them with my savings. I wouldn't have been able to do that if I did not have a stable job with a stable salary.
- Stable income lets you have a buffer for things and experiences that you love. You can occasionally fall off the wagon and afford impulsive purchases. Stability is what matters here. You know you would earn that back and not feel bad about spending too much. The nine to five salary is underrated. You realize the importance of it during unprecedented times. You will have a roof. You can afford food and a decent lifestyle for years to come, along with savings.

Yes, that is what a job in IT would give you.

Stability, for me, is mental peace. I remember the difficult times when I moved to the USA. As a full-time student, I didn't have much. I remember having three dollars left in my account after I had paid the advance for an apartment. I felt awful. I was 22.

I hated that feeling. I promised myself I would never let that happen again, and ever since then, my account balance has never been that low. I no longer have that stress. I have seen women buy super cute houses and establish businesses just with a stable nine to five job in the tech world.

Anonymous

What made you choose the Tech/Engineering field?

Growing up in an upper middle-class family with a very strict father, I always wanted to be independent and earn my money. So, immediately after graduating, I took up a job with the firm Virtusa, not knowing what I would be working on. Money was the only reason I started working but gradually I realized the importance of job, positions and different technologies and I started loving my work.

What career advice will you give to younger women out there?

You do not have to compete or prove anything to anyone except yourself. Work hard to achieve your goals. Don't stress over things you cannot control. It is your life, and you should be taking your own decisions. Create a better world for everyone out there. Good luck and lots of love!

****

Ruchie Raj Kumar, Project Coordinator, AI Hub (a facility run by the federal government to help SMEs adopt Artificial Intelligence) Canada.

What made you choose the Tech/Engineering field?

I've always been fascinated by tech, but never really wanted to be a programmer. So, I pursued Engineering in Computer Science to make sure I had a strong understanding of tech from an application perspective. I worked in IT for a while to know what starting ground up meant and learnt how teams were structured and work was allocated. I moved on to pursue my MBA to learn about how finance, operations, and project management worked at an enterprise level. This helped me understand the various industries better. As I learnt about all the different industries/sectors, I had a constant thought in my head and wondered how to apply tech to the various sectors and help with optimization. I realized my passion was working in the tech side of non tech industries. 7 years later, I am glad I decided to never get lost in the IT sector but to make sure I use my knowledge to help firms in the non-IT space adopt tech in some way or form to help optimize their processes or products.

What career advice will you give to younger women out there?

There is a preconceived notion, or a stereotype associated with the tech industry. Women are either always told that it is not for them or that it is too competitive for them. What women need instead, is to be told that they do not need to be like anyone specific to be in the tech industry and being in IT doesn't just mean coding. There needs to be awareness around the various roles one can pursue in the tech landscape. Always believe in the power of your dreams! Never let anyone tell you what you should be doing or should not be doing in your career. It is your career, not a community project! It must be your decision to fuel your passion, not theirs.

Chapter 3

IT ≠ Coding

According to the National Center for Women and Information Technology, in the United States of America, women comprised only 26 percent of the computing workforce in 2019. That percentage gave me chills. Can you imagine that?

Only 26 percent!!!!!!!!!!!!!!!!!!

That is it!!!!!!!!!!!!!!!!!!!!!!!!!!!!!!!!!!!

I wanted to know the reason for this number. I asked a few women from my network, and I realized that everyone mentioned one common thing. They believed that IT was tough and that it was just coding and sitting in front of a computer all day.

This is 100 percent *incorrect*.

I will be happy to break the news to you in one simple statement.

Coding is just one part of IT.

There are tons of different moving parts that make up a tech organization. Writing software in a programming language does not help with launching the app in the market.

Let's look at the example of baking a cake.

If I hand you a bowl and an oven, without any ingredients or instructions, would you be able to bake a cake for a bakery?

If you answered no to that question, then you understood my point.

To bake a cake, you need an oven and ingredients; you need measuring cups and spoons. You need to set the right temperature, and you need to measure and mix the ingredients as per the type of cake. You also need to preheat the oven and then set the batter in the pan. You would then put the mixture of wet and dry ingredients in the oven. After waiting for some time, you do the toothpick test to check if the cake was baked. You check if the cake has the right consistency, and then you take it out and wait for it to cool down. You go on to prepare the frosting. You might then decorate the cake, and after all this jazz, your cake will now be ready to sell.

An IT company is just that.

Whatever apps you use daily involve a hell of a lot more than just coding.

Creating and launching an app require many areas of responsibility, and some of these areas need skills that *do not involve coding.*

Let us go back to the example of the cake and compare it with an app that people use every day.

Think of any app, and now imagine that as a beautiful cake.

Our task is to figure out how to bake a perfect cake and sell it to our clients as per their preference.

Some people love chocolate, some love pineapple, and some love strawberry. These preferences would transform into requirements in a software company. In the IT world, there would be one department that talks to the clients and gets the app's requirements.

Next, we make a list of the ingredients for the cake, buy them, and measure them. In the tech industry, there is a team of people who determine the scope of the project. Scope? What do you mean by scope in terms of a cake, Sheekha? By this, I mean, is the cake going to be a simple cake or a four-tier cake? Determining the cake style is defining the scope of it. Scope determines the measurements for the cake.

Once we have the measurements, we need to figure out how much time we will need for the entire process. What are the risks, how much would it cost, and what other factors would be involved? We also need to know when to preheat the oven and the amount of time to bake.

All this happens in the software world with the app too. There are estimates and deadlines. Planning and discussions take place in the initial phases of the project.

Back to the cake. We determine the design of the cake. Do we need a square one, or a round one? Do we make a rectangle, unicorn shape, or a car-shaped cake? You might have little knowledge about the different kinds of shapes of cake pans and molds available in the market.

The occasion also plays a key role in determining the design of the cake. For example, you would not bake an Instagram logo cake for your 85-year-old grandmother, right?

The tech world is no different. An entire team of engineers spends time doing market research to conceptualize the design for an app. They generate ideas for design that target the right audience and the right age group in the market.

Now that you have all the raw materials and designs ready, you need to execute the plan. You will mix all the right ingredients and prepare the batter. This is an important step, but without the initial stage or the steps after this, your cake will never be ready.

Similarly, in the tech world, this is where programming comes into play. No one will become the next big thing in Silicon Valley by simply knowing how to code.

The point that I am trying to convey is that knowing how to prepare the batter does not mean you can bake a cake. It does not imply that you are ready to sell it to 50 different people every day.

Information technology is this big world with many different facets, and coding is one of them. Without these other parts and teams, it is nothing.

Getting back to our cake, after you have prepared the batter, you preheat the oven and bake it. Then you test it—the toothpick test.

An app also goes through rigorous cycles of testing. It is only after a lot of testing that an app would be ready for launch or go live.

Finally, the cake needs frosting and decorating to put it all together. In the tech industry, developers work on one feature at a time. They merge all the code and test it.

The cake needs care after the decoration is complete. You are now ready to put the cake up for display in your bakery. Eventually, you need to make sure you have the right-sized box to pack and deliver it.

In the tech world, this is where DevOps and hosting teams come into the picture. They make sure that the app features we worked on can be deployed and launched for the world to use it. A lot happens in the background.

So, ladies, if next time someone tells you they work in IT, do not imagine them sitting in front of a black screen with pink and green lines of code on it. Ask them which department, and what is their role in the tech world? Connect what they do to the steps in baking a cake, and you would instantly understand their role.

Be smart with your questions because now you know.

IT ≠ CODING.

Yay!!!!!

I spoke with all my friends and colleagues about this. They told me that if they had known all these different roles existed in IT, they would have chosen different streams and changed their course.

It was sad that nobody teaches this in the universities. They explain all about computers, how they work and what goes into it, but nobody teaches you the variety of roles, responsibilities, and skills required for these jobs.

This awareness is lacking in schools worldwide, and I personally believe this is the main cause of why the number of women in IT sucks.

It is a sh#t show because girls have no clue. How would you know when there isn't enough information on it? Why would you choose something that you are not aware of? I totally get it, but now you know.

I strongly believe that schools and colleges should not only encourage girls to take up coding classes but also teach them about other roles and jobs too. How can you get someone interested in eating a cake when they do not know all the different flavors that exist in the market? You cannot just show them a bare cake and ask them to start loving it.

Parents, too, I feel, should inquire more and force the universities to change their syllabus. Find people through social networking sites and help your kids choose what they want. First, however, you need to be aware that tech is not only coding. Find other resources that can guide your kids in the right direction.

Sara Mooney, Lead QA Engineer, USA.

What made you choose the Tech/Engineering field?

I slid in sideways! I was just a girl trying to be a salesperson (with crippling social anxiety) when a kind developer noticed I was very good at finding little glitches. She took me under her wing and bam...QA Engineer emerged.

What according to you is the main reason for less number of women in the tech/IT industry?

I truly believe it starts in high/secondary school where the computer clubs are male dominated and girls who show an interest in coding get nerd-shamed out of the room. We also do a terrible job of showing that a career in tech doesn't necessarily mean a development role. We need to show more people in general that QA (Quality Analyst), BA (Business Analyst) or other positions aren't a fallback job or a sign of engineering failure. These career choices are valid on their own.

I do agree with others who say that having a family can also be a deterrent. The 24/7 reputation of tech positions is toxic and keeps many people away. Deadlines are a thing, and innovation is important, but they should never get in the way of a healthy balance of work and life.

What career advice will you give to younger women out there?

Just go for it! Don't let your own impostor syndrome get in your way - you have a gift no one else has and the world needs you to share it.

******

Swetha Dhulipala, Software Developer, Wells Fargo, USA.

What made you choose the Tech/Engineering field?

When I was little, I always wondered how computers worked. When I was in 10th grade, we got internet connection at home and that helped me learn many amazing things, including how internet works. I always thought to myself how the world would be without tech. The amount of information that is being provided to us every day is vast and, I wanted to be a part of this amazing tech world too and contribute my part.

What according to you is the main reason for less number of women in the tech/IT industry?

Many women are not taking up STEM subjects thinking that they might not be able to perform as much as men, which is not true. In many cases women outperform men.

Also, many organizations think that women might not be able to contribute as much as men due to the notion that they are responsible for chores at home. They might also think about the possibility of women taking long maternity leaves which might lead to employing less women when compared to men.

What career advice will you give to younger women out there?

Start to explore all the possible options. Never think of a career path to be suitable specifically for men or women. Women can do anything men can and so do men. Just give your 100% to whatever you do. Never make anyone else decide your career path. It is your passion that drives you when you do the job. All the best.

Chapter 4

Women in Information Technology

Take a deep breath and think of social media and women. Ooo... I know your mind might have instantly drifted to Instagram and other apps for style, fashion, décor, and DIY. You are now thinking of #ootd and #friyay. Now, if I ask you to name a few influencers on Instagram or TikTok, you will most definitely come up with at least ten names. I know that was easy, right?

How many female CEOs can you name from the software world? I am aware that you know Mark Zuckerberg and Elon Musk for sure, but can you name any female counterparts?

You cannot. How can you?

Only 18 percent of CIO positions in the top 1000 companies were held by women in 2019.

18 percent. Not everyone in that 18 percent gets the hype from the media every day. They do not make the headlines unless something really bad happens.

According to data from the National Science Foundation, only 38 percent of women who majored in computer science are working in the field compared to 53 percent of men.

This is the most shocking number.

Another revealing fact that I read from the NCWIT fact sheet was this.

"Only 24 percent of women with an engineering degree still work in engineering, compared to 30 percent of men. This is a consistent trend that has been dubbed a 'leaky pipeline,' where it is difficult to retain women in STEM jobs once they've graduated with a STEM degree."

These numbers are appalling. We say we are modern and living the dream, but look around us. We are at a stage where only thirty-eight out of a hundred women with a computer science degree choose to work in the same field. We are not equal.

Thirty-eight percent is bad. It sucks.

Why?

Why is it that you know fewer women in this industry when compared to men? Why is it that girls do not want computer science as their major?

I blame the mindset. Girls are made to believe that they cannot build anything or create anything out of scratch. Long ago, they taught us to build dresses from scratch, and we excelled at it. They told us about the kitchen, and we learned how to cook meals from scratch, so why not the same thing with apps???

Why can't girls be asked to build apps from a young age? Why can't there be toys to build robots and apps for girls instead of dollhouses and kitchen sets? Why can't you dress up your daughter as a developer or an IT engineer for Halloween instead of a fairy princess? Even better, why not everything? Just because you are a software gal does not mean you have to hate pink or be a tomboy. Why can't you have the traits of a woman as well as an engineer?

It is a preconceived notion that IT is hard. Often it is assumed that building a PC, playing with computers, or creating a software application is difficult. Lack of awareness is the main cause.

How can you expect a fifteen-year-old girl to know how easy it is to be a QA engineer or a UX designer? It is not hard. You think it is hard because you do not know what it is or the terms intimidate you.

Did you think walking was hard? No, right? You learned to walk because you did it every day, and you started with a single step. Yes, you stumbled and fell many times, but you knew you had to do it. You realized that there is no way around it because you need to walk to survive. So, you learned it anyhow and moved up a level and then started running.

I don't know why but I am reminded of Forrest Gump—Run, Forrest, Run—okay, back to business.

Computers are the same. Your phone is a computer. Your laptop consists of apps that use different types of software. Engage your curious inner child and learn what a computer program does.

Hundreds of girls in third world countries are passing with an engineering degree every year. What is stopping you? If you live in one of the developed nations and do not want to be a part of the tech industry, I want to know why?

You might defend yourself by saying that it is expensive. To that, I say, every degree is expensive. There are student loans. I already told you that you would be able to pay it off with the salary you earn after landing an IT job.

What about the difficulty, you ask? If you do something daily, it will no longer be difficult. I am someone who learns by example, so when I read something new, I try to apply it to the real world. When I was in the tech world, I saw how real people used my projects in the real world. I was super excited, and that is what drives me to be the best at what I do.

There is a reason why there are many groups and conferences worldwide intended just for women in IT. It is due to the drastically low numbers. The statistics are lit and not in a good way.

If women can handle giving birth, the most difficult task on the planet, and they can survive menstrual periods, then learning about computers will be a piece of cake. Trust me. You just have to figure out where you fit and how your skills fit into the job description.

Being in the tech world does not make you a bore. It makes you a badass woman who thrives on challenges. I respect such women. I am not saying that you need to be smart to pursue a career in IT. All I am saying is, you must not act dumb either.

Women in tech face various challenges. I do not wish to scare you before you get into this world; instead, I want you to take this up with the "Hell yeah," attitude. Whenever someone told me I could not do it, I did that thing anyway to prove them wrong.

This book is one such example.

I spoke about millennials and test automation at five different conferences. I spoke about social media and smart women. Do you think this requires me to be smart or geeky? No. I just spoke the truth.

The buzzword today is social networking. We use this platform to showcase talents in every field. It is a must to be updated with the latest inventions and discoveries. Social networking sites have helped to prove to the world that women are not behind in any race. Statistics show an increase in the number of female users on these sites over men.

I believe that these platforms should be extensively used. Young students should be encouraged to explore various technical groups, which will result in a greater number of girls choosing computers as their career option.

I presented a paper a few years ago at the Missouri, Iowa, Nebraska, Kansas Women in Computing conference. Someone from the audience asked me, "How do you think this is possible through social networking sites?"

Here are a few steps that each one of us could implement almost daily to increase awareness and interest among young girls towards computing.

- Innovate to impact the world. I believe innovation is the key and can help students understand a complex computing concept in an easier fashion. I still remember the professor who taught computer organization at school. He asked us to imagine a semiconductor in the shape of a small chocolate cookie, and everyone in my class remembers that reference to date.
- Start various groups—big or small.
- Seminars and discussions should be conducted in schools.
- Use groups on social networking sites to promote IT as a career choice for girls.
- Spread awareness.
- Share posts on technology and make sure it reaches the target audience.
- Encourage young women to invent and discover new things.
- Talk. Talk to girls and learn what is stopping them from choosing tech careers. Suggest they join the technical groups and to explore the realm of technology.

If you have picked up this book, it means you are somewhat interested in learning about IT. It is appalling to see how few women are in the information technology industry; it's sad. Perhaps *you* can move the dial.

Women are the highest number of users of any social media apps. Women make or break a new social media app. Why settle for being just a user? Why not learn what goes into creating an app? Don't simply be an app consumer. Get into the roots and learn as much information you can about the configuration.

Create that awareness. Learn on your own. Google computers 101, and you will find many free courses online. Get a gist of it. Get a bird's overview of the course and do not get overwhelmed by the terminology. Once you learn to relate it to an existing app, trust me, you would be like, "Oooooohhhh, it means this?"

The tech world is sick. Initially, you will feel like an 80-year-old learning how to use TikTok, but once you get the hang of it, you will love it.

I promise.

Carrie Nelson, Executive Director/VP Client Services, USA.

What made you choose the Tech/Engineering field?

The need to bring the client facing skills to bridge technical and client business-facing teams. Technology is driving strategic decisions and growth for the organization; this focus and shift is opening more opportunities for client-facing roles within technology teams.

What career advice will you give to younger women out there?

Without senior women in IT leadership roles, there is a lack of mentors to help develop and sponsor women in a sector that has been male dominated.

- *Get involved in work that when you do it, you lose track of all time. When you are doing work that fulfills you, you are productive and successful.*
- *When you have been invited to a meeting, it means that you have knowledge, skills, and expertise that are needed. So, use your voice, and be comfortable in who you are and what you bring to a team and organization.*
- *When using your voice, you can say anything you want to say. It is all in how you say it.*
- *Surround yourself with the five people you want to become like. Look at who you are today and how you got there, while education and experience are important, you will find specific people played a significant part.*
- *Choose to be around individuals who are successful and that will elevate you.*

- *Don't just find a mentor, find a sponsor, someone who will advocate on your behalf. Decisions about your career and compensation are made when you are not in the room.*

******

Pavani, Portfolio Manager, Nisum, USA.

What made you choose the Tech/Engineering field?

I started as a developer and moved into product management and now my expertise lies in portfolio management. I like business, strategy and balance sheets. That was the reason why I moved to portfolio management role.

What career advice will you give to younger women out there?

Irrespective of gender, without a mentor, it takes good amount of time for anyone to realize what their calling is. We need consciously empowered people in any industry to drive change. You are not vulnerable because you are a woman. You are no less than a man. Look inside you and try to know yourself well. Write down what is the most important thing for you. Think what you can do for it and what you can't. Weigh in your morals, values, ethics, conviction and decide if you want to go that way and don't give up.

Section 2

Chapter 5

Finding Your Strength

By now, you are aware of the benefits of working in IT. You learned that IT is not all about programming languages, and you know we need more women here. Let's get to the interesting part now.

I want you to be able to reap the benefits of working in this field. I know you have it in you. So, in the upcoming chapters, I will help you figure out your strength and map it to the various jobs in the tech world.

It is a simple three-step process.

Know what you are good at.

Map it to an existing position.

Get lit!

Let us start by fishing for a skill. I believe everyone has a talent. Some are shy about it. I know that if you are the only person in a room, you will excel at your skill. I want you to take five minutes and reminisce.

Yes, I want you to go back to your childhood memories. I want you to come up with things or skills that you were good at. One skill is good. One or more is great.

Go.

You have five minutes. Go, go, go.

Talk to yourself and tell me what you liked doing as a child. What made you happy? What used to get a smile on your face? What was that one thing that you thought you could do forever and not get bored? What is that one thing that you can constantly do every single day and not crib about?

Do not worry. It can be ridiculous.

I assure you that you will find a job that matches your skill even if it is as weird as talking all day. Sshhh... I'll let you in on a secret. That is what the executives do all day. They talk and talk and talk and talk.

5

4

3

2

1

Okay, time is up. Do you have answers to all the above questions?

I remember saying earlier that you do not have to figure out everything at this stage, and that still holds true. If you did not come up with any skill you are good at, it is still okay. You will figure out something by the end of this book.

Back to the questions. What was your skill?

I bet some of the answers were drawing, painting, talking, sketching, writing, debating, arguing, cooking, managing, gaming, designing, finding faults, finding solutions, building something, doing puzzles, thinking, coming up with innovative and creative ideas, calculating, public speaking, math, leadership, playing an instrument, storytelling, acting, dancing and many more.

Phew. It sounds like a rap song, but I think I covered most of it.

All of these are useful skills. Skills that you will need to perform your daily job.

So, you ask, 'WTH? How can she say dancing? Dancing and IT??????? No way!!! That is insane."

Allow me to blow your mind. Think about this. Someone loved dancing and created this world-famous app, which is now used by 800 million people worldwide. One app that forced the most powerful economies to ban it!

TikTok.

So, how can you say that dancing and IT do not go hand in hand? Go on and flip the page. I will wait for your comeback—that is, when you have one—# burn.

Aakruthi Vaishnavi, Senior researcher, Magellan Life Sciences., India.

What made you choose the Tech/Engineering field?

I was always inclined towards experiments and bringing out something new through trial-and-error method. I took it rather seriously and pursued Master's in Biotechnology, giving me ample opportunity to fuse biology with technology for inventions that are needed in the present health situation of the world.

What according to you is the main reason for less number of women in the tech/IT industry?

The social bias that women are less competent in showing progress/success by labelling marriage + children breaks as a major roadblock.

I do not like the stereotype that men should work while women can take a backstep and take care of the family. The society estimates skills traditionally. They find women to be delicate for certain job, emotional for some other and thus somehow stop them climbing the professional growth ladder smoothly.

What career advice will you give to younger women out there?

There is no man or woman when it comes to ambition. The opportunity to change the world one step at a time, the joy of being financially independent and the confidence it contributes to the overall personality is something that should not be compromised or missed. So, no matter how whacky an idea or how tedious a job, if it's something that drives you sleepless, then you should pursue it with all your heart and only listen to the heart alone. Society is just a fraction of the world. Having a successful career will eliminate everything the society has type casted for centuries!

****

Sherri Wahl, Sr. Software QA Engineer, TEAM Software, USA.

What made you choose the Tech/Engineering field?

I started out as a receptionist and backup to our helpdesk manager which was only temporary until I found a direction I wanted to go within the organization. I went to help the QA team and never left. I had a great role model that mentored me and taught me how to write automation code.

What career advice will you give to younger women out there?

Don't be intimidated with working in IT. Most males have been great role models for me and are willing to share knowledge.

****

Smitha Appukuttan Hervey, Software Engineer, USA.

What made you choose the Tech/Engineering field?

My awesome Indian family put it in my head that I was going to be an Engineer when I grew up and I followed the path. Though I have no regrets, I wish they would have instilled the desire in me to be a doctor instead.

What career advice will you give to younger women out there?

In my opinion, when a child is young, parents play a major role in shaping the child's future choices. You can be in any profession that you choose if you are willing to put it in the work.

Chapter 6

Find Your Niche

Google describes a niche as "a comfortable or suitable position in life or employment."

You know how sometimes your gut says you can do it, envision it, but reality turns out to be completely different? I want you to know what makes you feel that way.

It doesn't matter if your gut feeling tells you to become an astronaut or design the world's best house. What is your gut feeling? What is the thing that you know you will be amazing at? What generates that passion in you?

Disclaimer—you are allowed to be ridiculous because it means you are on the right track. If you feel it is ridiculous and you think it is insane to pursue it, chances are, you are going to excel at it. It is supposed to evoke that scary sensation in you. That will be your niche.

I want to say this out loud, "We should start normalizing average."

Okay, that might have felt weird; try it again #normalizebeingaverage. I want to be able to live in a world where being average is fine. I want to normalize the thought that having an average salary and a decent lifestyle is way more peaceful than working you're a#& off twenty-four hours a day and not spending time with family or friends. That money is of no use if you cannot spend it on yourself or people who matter to you.

It is trash. Period.

Having said that, a comfortable life does not come instantly. Job satisfaction is a major underrated factor in the tech world. Yes, there are people like me who love their jobs, but many more do not love their jobs. They survive the nine to five rut only to be able to pay their bills and expenses.

I do not want you to be that person who gets into IT just to earn money. I want you to get into tech for the right reasons. I asked you to go through the exercise of finding your skills because I believe that job satisfaction cannot be achieved if you can just perform certain tasks. You need to learn to enjoy doing those tasks every day.

For example, I can type. I can type all day long, but if you ask me to look at papers and type eight hours a day for the rest of my life, I will not do it. I will not prefer this job, because I do not enjoy it. Even though it would pay my bills, I will not do it because it does not make me happy. Just because I can do a task does not mean I will be happy doing it every day.

I want you to think the same way about technology. Just because you can get a job in IT with a four-year computer science degree, you don't have to force yourself into a tech job because I told you it could pay bills. I want you to be eventually happy with your job and love it.

I am a QA Engineer, and I love finding bugs. Bugs in the tech world are issues and faults in the software. For example, the password requirements on a website say your password must contain six letters, one number, and a capital letter. If you can create a password without a capital letter, then that is a bug.

I love testing. The reason I love my job is because I get to find faults. I am not proud of it, but it makes me good at my job. I do not like to call it finding faults. Let me rephrase it; my attention to detail is immaculate—sounds way more sophisticated now, right.

I love my job because I found a space where I could employ what I am good at and excel at it. I made sure I was current with the latest in the testing world by attending testing conferences. One day I found myself on the stage, presenting a topic at testing conferences. The public speaking was possible because I found a job that made me happy; a job that kept me curious—thus attending conferences and getting noticed—and most importantly, a job that I found satisfying.

I earn enough money. The only difference between the other person and me in the next cubicle is that I love my job. I do not have #mondayblues. Even though I look forward to the happy hours on Fridays, I still do not regret being in IT for even a single second because I designed my job around my skill.

I want you, or your daughter, your niece, your sister to find their niche too. I want you to have that comfortable and suitable position in employment and life.

Find your niche, even if it is scary, unimaginable, and stupid. It is fine. Because it is yours, it is *your* niche.

If I had told my mom that I want to travel and earn money, she would have laughed at me, but right now, travel bloggers are the actual Instagram rock stars. That is their niche. They like that kind of life. They find peace and comfort in traveling to different countries, staying in a variety of places, and exploring while earning money. They love what they do.

You need to find your niche too. Right now. It is never too late.

So, what is your niche?

Leanna Escobar, Technical Writer, Phynd Technologies, Inc., USA.

What made you choose the Tech/Engineering field?

A temporary contract opportunity came up to build a knowledge base and a client support system. Then the opportunity expanded to a full-time salaried position to create recurring release notes and other technical documentation for clients as well as for internal training purposes. I work with the Product Manager and with most teams in the company to ensure that documentation reflects updates to the product as well as aligns with marketing campaigns. I also assist with roadmap planning and requirement preparation to ensure the product has the most effective UI design as well as consistency across the application and platform.

What according to you is the main reason for less number of women in the tech/IT industry?

Lack of exposure to different positions and areas of work to consider when choosing an educational or vocational path or when choosing your life's work. There should be more promotion of women in tech because it is an industry that is usually more flexible for that ideal family life balance.

What career advice will you give to younger women out there?

Be curious. Try new things all the time. You're never too old and it's never too late. Discover what your interests are. Find what makes you feel inspired or happy. Then choose what program of study or line of work you'd like to pursue. In any industry there is a need for women with both technical and non-technical skills. Who says you cannot have both or can't pursue both?

****

Aanchal Sharma, Software Development Engineer, Jio Platforms Limited., India.

What made you choose the Tech/Engineering field?

Technology always fascinated me. I aspire to solve problems and impact the masses positively. Technology is a great domain to achieve this. Hence, I am an engineer working on building solutions to problems in order to ease the life of mankind.

What according to you is the main reason for less number of women in the tech/IT industry?

Women are considered less competitive than men. **According to a survey on GitHub, the tendency of acceptance of code is more by women only if they hide their gender. Women are not given due recognition not because they are incapable of delivering tasks but because there is a cultural prejudice which needs global attention.

**Female led technology businesses achieve on an average 35% more ROI than those run by men. Hence, a shift in the mindset which is prevailing since ages is necessary.

What career advice will you give to younger women out there?

Women are multitaskers and can achieve anything they aspire for. There is a dire need of women in Technology industry and hence we see a boost in the diversity and inclusion programs. It means that changes are being made to accept more women in tech. A woman should never underestimate herself and should be in the forefront to grab opportunities. Take up responsibilities and go beyond to achieve your dreams.

**Check Appendix for references.

Section 3

Chapter 7

Mapping Skills to Real-World Jobs

Presuming that by now, you have a hint of what you are good at, let's move on to the next step. I would now like to present the various job titles and positions in the tech world that do and do not involve coding so that you can map your skills to the job duties.

For the scope of this book, I will only list out the jobs pertaining to the software engineering organizations and software development companies.

Intro to Areas of Computing:

Computer Science and Engineering is a broad area of science and engineering and involves the following and more:

Algorithms

Hardware

Software

Networking

Artificial Intelligence

Cryptography

Security

Data Structures

Computer Architecture

Graphics

Machine Learning

Bioinformatics

Computer science is considered a part of a family of five separate yet interrelated disciplines: computer engineering, computer science, information systems, information technology, and software engineering.

If we choose only computer science, then it involves the following:

Algorithms and complexity

Architecture and organization

Computational science

Graphics and visual computing

Human-computer interaction

Information management

Intelligent systems

Networking and communication

Operating systems

Parallel and distributed computing

Platform-based development

Programming languages

Security and information assurance

Software engineering

Social and professional issues

Software Engineering is one sector in the vast world of Computers.

Software Engineering comes into the picture when we discuss apps such as Instagram, Twitter, TikTok, Google maps, Skype, Zoom, etc. However, now the market has changed.

Earlier, we had apps that could only be used on a desktop or laptop, but now, apps are developed for wearables like Apple Watch, Fitbit, etc. A smartwatch is a wearable computer in the form of a watch.

Everything is a program. From something as simple as setting your alarm to a complex process of recording your sleep quality is a set of programs. It is an amalgamation of rules and design with code and technology, all working in unison to provide you with the latest tech in the market.

Software engineering is the discipline concerned with applying theory, knowledge, and practice to building reliable software systems that satisfy the computing requirements of customers and users. It applies to small, medium, and large-scale computing systems and organizations.

Remember the example of the cake. Just like the different stages in baking, software development, too, is a process. It is a cycle that involves multiple steps at multiple stages.

The software engineering process is usually described as consisting of several phases, called a life cycle, variously defined but generally consisting of requirements development, analysis and specification, design, construction, validation, deployment, operation, and maintenance.

Before diving into the areas and positions in a typical software development organization, I would like you to get familiar with the different domains.

Think of domains as different shops in a mall. For example, if you need to withdraw money from your bank account, you will not walk into a shoe store or a clothing store. You go to a bank or an ATM. Similarly, with computers, there are different industries, and all these industries require software applications to help achieve their goal.

Eight industries for software development are:

Retail

Healthcare

Finance

Business/IT services

Research and development

Government and defense

Tech industry

Entertainment

Each industry requires different types of people and different skill sets. Consider, for example, gaming. The skill sets needed for the gaming industry is completely different when compared to other domains.

Irrespective of the industry you work in, the core software development cycle and processes used will be the same. The end product or service might vary, but the process is the same. Agile is one such example.

In the agile teams, all the releases occur at a set interval and follow a release cycle. A small part of the project is designed, developed, tested, hosted, and shipped to the client. This cycle is repeated every two or three weeks until the end-user is ready to use the final application. Most of the jobs in the software industry have similar responsibilities and duties.

The IT Girl

Pam Sampson, Software Engineer, D3 Banking-NCR, USA.

What made you choose the Tech/Engineering field?

My interest peaked in high school when I started creating websites for the school paper. I liked that the work I produced was something functional that everyone could see and use. I decided before going to college I wanted a degree in computer science.

Freshman year of college, a male, older than me told me that I would be weeded out the first year. That doubt from a complete stranger drove me hard.

After undergrad school, I went on to get my master's. I was super intimidated to get a job. The terms used in job descriptions were the ones that I had only maybe heard of. The work I had done for my thesis helped me get my first job. I have been a software developer ever since.

What according to you is the main reason for less number of women in the tech/IT industry?

The thought that getting a computer related degree will be hard and I don't just mean academically but socially as well. If you feel like you don't fit in it will be hard to socialize with others. You won't have friends in the program and therefore no one to go to when you need help. That puts you at a disadvantage and can be isolating. That is not an attractive career choice.

College is about meeting people and being in a program that is associated with being a ""nerd"" does not attract people coming straight out of high school.

What career advice will you give to younger women out there?

It is hard to think about financial stability at a young age but being able to support yourself gives you so much control of your life. I am free to do whatever I want whenever I want. I have job security during this crazy pandemic. You can see a list of available positions that exist on the internet and feel safe. Even if your first passion isn't technology, it is literally integrated in everything we do. Having an educational background will have an advantage regardless of the position.

****

Mounica, Team Lead, Infor Pvt ltd, India.

What made you choose the Tech/Engineering field?

Just like a casual and competitive engineer, I wanted to earn money. I worked hard for interviews and ended up in this wide tech field. I marvel at how my views changed. I'm independent now and absolutely love my job more than anything. (not more than my daughter, of course.)

What career advice will you give to younger women out there?

Do what you like but take the right decision with the help of others which doesn't hurt your loved ones further in your career. Don't let culture and attitude of few educated illiterates hinder your growth.

****

Priscilla Victor, Sr Software Engineer, Tech Mahindra India.

What made you choose the Tech/Engineering field?

I always wanted to become a doctor. Since my family could not afford it, I chose engineering. I didn't think of changing my field ever because I got a job offer before I graduated. This job is convenient and financially secure.

What career advice will you give to younger women out there?

Analyze your interests. Research more and get inspired. Know exactly who you want to be. Never ever compromise on your dream. No field is higher than the other field. Every field has its prominence. You may receive backlash but remember that should only make you stronger. Change your path only if you want to.

****

Mounika Yerramsetty, Application Developer, Mutual of Omaha, USA

What made you choose the Tech/Engineering field?

Like many 90s kids, I grew up playing pc games, using paint and Word Art for writing my name in different styles. That is how my interest began. I was inspired by my sister and friends who landed great offers in software companies. During high school, I always dreamt of wearing an ID card and working with tech in a big software firm. After undergrad, I pursued my masters in USA.

I had to work on my communication skills, confidence levels, and a few technical concepts for every interview. I did not get through first four interviews but kept applying for job openings until I

69

landed an entry level developer job at Nelnet. 4 years later, I knew I needed to advance in my career and so, I enrolled in some more courses and certifications. Today, I am a senior developer at Mutual of Omaha. If I can achieve my dream, then so can you.

What career advice will you give to younger women out there?

Dream big about your career when you are young. When you grow up, don't give up on them just because you were told to, or your priorities changed. Don't stop because of difficult situations or due to change in status. (Staying in a relationship or getting married.) You can do a lot with your thoughts, actions and time. Also, take care of your health while you get busy shaping your career.

Chapter 8

Intro to Job Positions

It is time to unveil the core of this book. This chapter contains the average salaries and job duties for roles in a typical software development organization.

The titles could be confusing at first. To make it easier, I have divided the roles into dedicated areas of a company. They fit a typical organizational structure at any given software company. These jobs belong to different departments and have different responsibilities, but they are interrelated and interdependent.

The salaries shown are the average annual salaries in the United States as per the Bureau of Labor Statistics in May 2019. Unless mentioned otherwise, all the positions require a bachelor's degree in computer science or a related field.

Software Engineer

Software developers are responsible for the development, design, and implementation of software applications. They develop software based on their programming skills. Although writing code is not their priority, developers must have a strong background in computer programming. They design, test, and develop software to meet the project's requirements. Developers create the games that you play on Ps4, Xbox, or PC, and the apps you use on your phone or TV.

Average Salary:

Median average salary for a software developer is $107,510.

The lowest ten percent earned less than $64,240, and the highest ten percent earned more than $164,590.

Skill Set:

Strong programming skills, strong technical knowledge, analytical skills, communication skills, and problem-solving skills.

QA Engineer

Quality Assurance engineers and QA analysts are responsible for testing the application. There are manual QA engineers as well as Automation QA engineers. Once the development of a feature is complete, the QA engineers perform various levels of testing and identify potential issues with the software.

Consider, for example, the login button. Typically, you would enter your email address or username. But, when you are testing login functionality, you test by entering numbers instead of email or invalid characters. Test cases are created to check if the functionality adheres to the requirements and is ready for the end-user.

This is my favorite role. It does not involve heavy coding. Every application requires testing, and QA engineers are responsible for the overall quality of the product.

Average Salary:

Median average salary for a software quality assurance engineer is $93,710. The lowest ten percent earned less than $55,180, and the highest ten percent earned more than $147,670.

Skill Set:

Highly detail-oriented, communication skills, time management skills, and ability to work as a part of a team.

If you have good observation skills and if you are detail-oriented or find yourself correcting things, you should consider being a QA engineer. Manual QA engineer positions do not require programming skills.

Scrum Master

The scrum master is the scrum team leader and is responsible for championing a project, providing guidance to the team and product owners. A scrum master ensures that team members follow all the agile practices.

The scrum master addresses all facets of the agile development process and serves the business and the team at large. He or she facilitates communication and collaboration between these elements. They lead the daily standups and sprint planning meetings that require effective planning. They coach the entire team to follow agile principles and cause changes that increase the productivity of the team.

Average Salary:

In 2018, Glassdoor research included Scrum Master in their list of highest paying jobs ranking at number twenty with a median salary of $98,239.

Per a 2019 survey, women represent 29 percent of the scrum masters; the remaining percentage are men.

LinkedIn also included Scrum Master in its 2019 Most Promising Jobs list.

Skill Set:

Conflict resolution skills, coaching agile practices, removing impediments, facilitating meetings, communication channel, servant leader, enforcing rules, leadership skills, and organizational skills.

Are you known to resolve conflicts among your friends? Do you like to streamline processes or find yourself being a middleman in most of the conversations? If yes, then you should give this a try. If you can handle multiple projects and teams, then you will be perfect as a scrum master.

You will enforce many new ideas for the entire software development team. You will learn to be a good listener. This job does not require you to be technical. It has nothing to do with coding. This role entails the smooth functioning of the team and organization at large. It is an important role at a software company.

IT Business Analyst

Business analysts help guide businesses by improving processes, products, services, and software through data analysis. These agile workers straddle the road between IT and business. They bridge the gap and improve efficiency. Business analysts are responsible for creating an in-depth analysis of the business, outlining problems, opportunities, and solutions. They are involved in budgeting, forecasting, planning, monitoring, variance analysis, and reporting. They do a fine job of defining business requirements and reporting them back to stakeholders.

Average Salary:

The average salary for a business analyst is $91,160. The lowest ten percent earned $49,700, and the highest ten percent earned $154,310.

Skill Set:

- Analytical skills are a must for this role. You should be able to interpret information and use their findings to form proposals.
- Communication skills are required to convey information clearly in both writing and speaking. Analysts also need good listening skills to know an organization's problems and recommend appropriate solutions.
- Interpersonal skills are needed since business analysts work with managers and other employees of the organization. They provide top-quality consulting services, and they work with the team towards achieving the organization's goals.

- Problem-solving skills
- Time-management skills are the most important skills needed.

If you communicate exceptionally and have strong analytical skills, then this is the right position for you. This job, too, does not involve any coding.

Systems Analyst

Computer systems analysts help organizations run computer technology effectively. They incorporate technology into current systems after doing cost-benefit analysis. They determine whether it is financially sound and if it will serve the entity efficiently. They research and evaluate new technologies. They need to consult with clients to identify the organizational needs of IT systems. Systems analysts oversee installations, test systems, and train users.

Average Salary:

The average salary for systems analysts is $88,740. The lowest ten percent earned less than $54,360, and the highest ten percent earned more than $142,220.

Skill Set:

Problem-solving skills, critical thinking, communication, and reading comprehension skills are a must. Computer systems analysts must read manuals and technical reports to keep up with advances and implement new technology that meets employers' or clients' needs. Writing and creativity are also needed.

If you like to set up new hardware and software, this will be the right fit for you. If you love learning new technology and solving problems, then a systems analyst position is the way to go. No programming skills are needed for this role.

Technical Writer

Technical writing involves preparing instruction manuals, how-to guides, journal articles, and other supporting documents. Technical writers communicate complex and technical information more easily. They prepare technical documentation, instructions manual for both internal users and end-users. A major task for them is standardizing and improving content.

Average Salary:

The average salary for a technical writer is $72,850.

Skill Set:

Technical writers must take complex, technical information and simplify it for their colleagues and consumers with non-technical backgrounds.

Apart from keen attention to detail, imagination is also needed. Technical writers create detailed instructions for others to follow. They must be able to think about a procedure or product in the way a non-technical person would.

Technical writers must be able to work well with others. They are almost always part of a team with other writers, designers, editors, illustrators, and the technical engineers whose information they are explaining. Many technical writers need a background in engineering or computer science to excel at this job.

If your strength lies in writing and presenting information in a simple manner, then a technical writer is the perfect position for you.

Graphic Designer

Graphic designers are the creative staff that formulate and pitch graphic concepts to clients. They are responsible for developing, designing, and producing graphic art that meets the client's demands. They should be adept at meeting tight deadlines and staying within the allotted budget.

Designers are usually proficient in programs such as Adobe Illustrator, Photoshop, and InDesign. They have a good knowledge of typography, color, and production. This position involves continuous learning to update skills and be on par with current trends in the industry.

Average Salary:

According to the US Bureau of Labor Statistics, the midpoint salary for graphic designers is $52,110.

Skill Set:

The skills needed vary from creativity and versatility to deep knowledge of branding and marketing techniques.

You'll need a strong sense of concept development and problem-solving. Research and presentation abilities are needed in a graphic designer. Good verbal and written communication skills are vital.

If you love being creative and you like thinking out of the box, then graphic designing should be ideal for you. If you love designing, drawing, or working with images, then this job is for you.

UX Engineer

UX stands for user experience. UX engineers are the unicorns of the product world. They create designs, put them in the right place, and even do growth hacking along with user research. UX engineers are extremely high in-demand at startups and big tech companies like Google and Facebook.

They partner with researchers and designers to define and deliver new features. UX engineers are known to translate concepts into living, breathing prototypes. They work to deliver the perfect experience by collaborating the design with engineering. They deal with human-computer interaction daily. For example, the Instagram logo or the placement of the icons on any app is handled by a team of UX designers and engineers.

Average Salary:

The average median salary for a UX engineer is $107,670.

Inexperienced UX engineers can expect to make the least when they start. For example, a UX engineer with one year of experience at a company with twenty-five employees in Raleigh, NC, can expect to make about $76,305 on average. On the other hand, an engineer with ten or more years of experience working at a large firm in San Francisco can make between $145,000 and $170,000.

Skill Set:

The primary skills needed for this job are auxiliary skills and other qualities besides the UX design expertise. These are often skills that go hand-in-hand with your design knowledge and creativity. UX designers who have some idea about analytics, team building, or psychology and research can often negotiate higher salaries since these assets make them a more attractive candidate for the job.

If you are fueled by creativity and crave innovation in design, then UX engineer is the perfect job for you. Consider this role if you can present visually appealing and efficient designs.

Data Analyst

A data analyst loves data. Data analysts interpret data and turn it into information that offers many ways to improve a business. They play an important role that affects business decisions. Data analysts gather information from various sources. They begin by studying and analyzing patterns and trends. Once the data has been gathered and interpreted, the data scientist reports back what has been found in a comprehensive study.

Average Salary:

According to the University of Wisconsin, an average data scientist earns $113,000. The salaries range from $50,000 and $95,000.

Skill Set:

Strong analytical skills, along with an inclination to solve problems, is mandatory. Attention to detail is another must since this job involves studying huge amounts of data. Ability to generate reports from large data sets is preferred.

If you love playing with numbers and get intrigued by the sheer amount of data available, then data analyst is your ideal role.

Social Media Manager

Social media managers need more than just a creative mind. They should have the ability to play with words, images, videos, and turn them into compelling content. Thorough knowledge of the most popular social platforms is mandatory. Twitter, Facebook, and LinkedIn are just a toe in the water.

Keeping up with the latest developments means snapping, yelping, or shortening with bitly. They need to be able to figure out the insights and gain engagements. In a software company, this role mostly requires implementing innovative social media strategy, developing brand awareness, generating inbound traffic, and encouraging product adoption. They create and publish content and maintain relationships with user communities on many platforms.

Average Salary:

The starting salary for social media managers is $57,750.

Skill Set:

High levels of diplomacy online and offline is a required skill for this position. Knowledge of SEO (search engine optimization) is key. Social media managers today have a knack for generating highly creative campaigns. They are skilled enough to collaborate with internal marketing and public relations teams to support their respective missions, ensuring consistency in voice and cultivating an engaged social media community for the company.

Do you have a gift for storytelling? Can you develop strategies around the latest social media trends? If you answered yes to the questions, then this is your ideal position.

DevOps Engineer

DevOps engineers have a combination of skills that enable them to overcome the barriers between software development and operations teams. They play a key role during a code release. The demand for professionals with DevOps skills is on the rise. The demand increases as the frequency of code deployments increase. They achieve the elimination of silos, which leads to better process management.

There is no one set career path for becoming a DevOps engineer. A software developer who is interested in networking operations and deployment can choose to become a DevOps engineer.

Average Salary:

Data from PayScale shows that in the US, DevOps engineers earn between $91,000 and $155,000.

Skill Set:

Adept knowledge of software development, IT systems, and operations is required. You should be flexible with higher testing and deployment frequencies and should be able to operate in production environments. The ability to use efficient automation tools is preferred.

Project Manager

Project managers in the information technology (IT) world are tasked with planning projects. They ensure that these projects are executed on time and follow the roadmap through every stage of the process. This job requires daily evaluation of employees, as well as leadership and motivation skills to be successful.

IT project managers must ensure that team members have the same shared vision and goals for projects. Problem-solving is necessary when projects are not going as planned.

Average Salary:

The average pay for an IT project manager is $109,743.

Skill Set:

Excellent communication and negotiating skills are needed. Project managers spend most of their time collaborating with the team and reporting progress or problems to clients; hence, verbal and written skills are a must.

Project managers need to display the ability to lead and motivate a team. Conflict resolution skills and timely engagements for project deliveries are critical. They need to be organized professionally. It is important to develop an effective organizational system.

If you have leadership, management, and exceptional organizational qualities, you can start to think about being a project manager. If you are often called to give presentations and if you are comfortable speaking in front of large groups of people, you will fit well as a project manager.

Client Manager

Client managers are liaisons between a company and its clients. They are responsible for ensuring excellent customer service and client satisfaction. Managing client relationships, developing plans, and delivering proposals are key tasks of a client manager. They are the face of a software company for a particular client. Everything from the internal teams is communicated to the client by a client manager.

Average Salary:

The average salary for client relationship managers, per PayScale, is $62,873.

Skill Set:

Knowledge of or experience with working in the customer service, sales, or business development area is preferred. Strong communication and negotiation skills, as well as solid presentation skills, are required.

Many but not all employers require client managers to have a bachelor's degree in business, computer information systems, or a related field. You should be able to demonstrate abilities to exceed target revenue goals, provide excellent customer service, build long-term relationships, and represent the company effectively.

Client Support Specialist

Computer network support specialists are also called technical support specialists. They analyze, troubleshoot, and evaluate computer network problems. They play a major role in the routine maintenance of their company's networks. They are responsible for performing file backups on the network. They also perform regular maintenance checks for an organization's disaster recovery efforts. Client support specialists often assist users through phone, email, or in-person visits. They generally work under network and computer systems administrators.

Average Salary:

The median annual wage for computer user support specialists was $52,270 in May 2019. The lowest ten percent earned less than $32,330, and the highest ten percent earned more than $88,470.

Skill Set:

Need to be attentive to cater to the customer's problems and diagnose them. Good communication skills to walk the customers through the problem-solving steps. Solid skills needed to set up and repair computer equipment.

Information Security Analyst

Security is one of the major concerns for any tech company. The risk increases with various factors. An information security analyst plans out security measures to protect a company's computer network and systems. As cyberattacks increase, the demand for security analysts increases. IT security analysts are heavily involved with creating disaster recovery plans, a procedure that IT employees follow in case of emergency. The plan involves preventive measures such as regularly copying and transferring data to an offsite location. IT security analysts mitigate risks and have plans in place to restore proper functioning after a disaster.

Average Salary:

$99,730 is the median salary for an information security analyst.

Skill Set:

Analytical skills are as important as are problem-solving skills. Information security analysts must be detail-oriented since they carefully investigate any irregularities to determine if the networks have been compromised.

Ingenuity is a must. If you think you can try to outthink cybercriminals and invent new ways to protect systems and networks, then this role is for you.

Sales Engineer

Sales engineers in the technology sector play a vital role. They sell complex technological products and services to other businesses. They talk to customers and determine their requirements. They secure contracts by selling software products and services.

Average Salary:

The median annual wage for sales engineers was $103,900 in May 2019.

Skill Set:

A bachelor's degree in engineering or a related field is typically needed for this role. To be successful as a sales engineer, a combination of technical knowledge of the products or services they are selling is needed along with strong interpersonal skills. You must have excellent presentation and communication skills to offer services to existing and prospective clients.

Being able to sell a product and upsell a service is a gift. If you are amazing at sales, then this is the right role for you. Selling software is a challenge and super fun at any organization.

Database Administrator

Database administrators (DBA) work with the database of an organization that requires an administrator. They oversee complex systems and monitor database performance by using specialized types of software to store and organize a company's data. They deal with a variety of information, from confidential financial numbers to payroll data to customer shipping records. This is a crucial role because a DBA makes sure that data is kept secure from unauthorized access, accidental loss, or corruption.

Average Salary:

The median annual salary for a database administrator is $93,750. The top ten percent earned more than $148,060, and the bottom ten percent earned less than $51,800.

Skill Set:

Being detail-oriented is a top skill needed to be a DBA. Top-notch analytical skills and communication skills are needed to deal with information coming from a variety of sources. A minor error can cause major problems, and a database administrator should be efficient at problem-solving.

For example, if customer credit card information gets mixed up, it can cause people to be charged for purchases they did not make. It is the job of the DBA to figure out the bug and resolve the problem.

Infrastructure Engineer

Infrastructure engineers are held responsible for designing, building, deploying, and maintaining the IT infrastructure. They typically are known for updating and using the latest technology to support any size of business operation. Infrastructure engineers have to ensure that IT systems function efficiently. This involves working with internet connections, virtualization of platforms, and storage area networks.

Average Salary:

The average salary for infrastructure engineers is $79,480.

Skill Set:

Knowledge about network and security concepts, SAN technology, storage, tuning techniques, and system performance configuration is preferred. Exposure to other areas such as TCP/IP environment, virtualization technologies, OS performance monitoring, Apache Web Server, and Tomcat Server is an advantage.

If you are intrigued by the infrastructure of towns and cities, you will absolutely love learning about computer infrastructure. If you generally like knowing how an entire city is connected and the role a good infrastructure plays, then you will enjoy learning about computer networks. This job would be a perfect fit for you. The terms sound super complicated, but computer networking is a lot more interesting. The advancements in this field are astonishing.

Network Administrator

Network administrators provide their expertise in managing an organization's computer networks. They are also referred to as systems administrators, IT managers, or LAN administrators. They typically organize, install, and provide support for these systems.

Average Salary:

The average salary for a network administrator is $112,690. The lowest ten percent earned less than $64,770, and the highest ten percent earned more than $168,390.

Skill Set:

Need to be familiar with creating plans and layouts for data communication networks. Expertise in local area networks (LANs), wide area networks (WANs), and intranets is preferred. You should be able to upgrade hardware, such as routers, adaptors, and software, such as network drivers, as needed to support computer networks. You should regularly research new networking technologies to determine what would best support their organization.

Do the terms LAN and WAN get you excited? If yes, then this will definitely be your cup of tea.

Systems Engineer

Systems engineers impact a tech company by designing, implementing, and maintaining the infrastructure necessary to run web applications. Their job duties include installing, supporting software, and debugging systems. System engineers are specialists who perform high-level root cause analysis. They offer recovery and preventive measures.

Average Salary:

According to the Robert Half technology 2020 salary guide, the salary midpoint for a systems engineer is $106,000.

Skill Set:

Flexibility and the ability to thrive in complex and changing environments is a must. A solid mix of technical and nontechnical skills is required. A candidate with good analytical and troubleshooting skills is preferred.

Do you want to be part of software development but also have a desire to work with hardware? If so, a job as a systems engineer may be the ideal hybrid job for you.

Applications Support Analyst

An Application Support Analyst plays a major role in assisting in areas of applications programming. These areas include testing, design, and analysis. These analysts support the team responsible for a subset of business systems applications. The main responsibility of an application support analyst is to assist in the formulation of procedures and best practices for the end-users.

Average Salary:

The average salary for an Application Support Analyst is $69,600. It ranges between $57,200 and $77,900.

Skill Set:

An ability to work with cross-functional teams and juggle multiple projects is necessary. In addition to excellent written, verbal skills, high attention to detail, and leadership skills are required. Analysts typically work under the close direction of senior personnel in the functional area. Knowledge of scripting, coding, and application software is preferred.

AI Engineer

Artificial Intelligence is the buzzword today. This industry is massive and remains to be the topmost field in terms of technological innovations. The term AI is broad and covers several disciplines and tasks. It includes natural language generation, comprehension, speech recognition, chatbots, machine learning, decision management, deep learning, biometrics, text analysis, and processing. Each discipline requires a certain level of specialization. For example, Amazon Echo and Google Home are AI-powered devices.

AI engineers build models using machine learning algorithms. They incorporate deep learning neural networks to draw business insights, which are used to make business decisions. AI engineers utilize various tools and techniques to process data, develop and maintain artificial intelligent systems.

Average Salary:

The average salary for an artificial intelligence engineer in the San Francisco area ranges from approximately $134,135 to $169,930.

The average pay for an AI programmer is around $100,000 to $150,000. To make the big money, you want to be an AI engineer.

Skill Set:

According to The New York Times, there are fewer than 10,000 qualified AI specialists in the world. Element AI, a Montreal company that consults on machine learning systems, published a report in 2020 that suggesting only 22,000 Ph.D.-level computer scientists in the world are capable of building AI systems.

A heavy range of various programming languages is required for an AI Engineer. Some of them are Machine learning, Python, R language, Hadoop, Big Data, Java, Spark, and SAS. This is a wide range of skills, and none of them are learned overnight.

If reading this job description sparked a fire in you, then I would strongly recommend planning for a computer science degree with a specialization in AI.

Machine Learning Engineer

Artificial intelligence is the goal of a machine learning engineer. Machine learning engineers are responsible for programming machines to perform specific tasks. They feed data into AI models and create programs that enable machines to take action without being directed.

A self-driving car is an example of a system that a machine learning engineer would work on. Machine learning engineers develop services from customized news feeds to tailored web searches. They work with huge quantities of information and perform complex modeling on data sets.

Average Salary:

The average salary of a machine learning engineer is $111,141.

Skill Set:

Exceptional mathematical skills, paired with strong analytical skills, along with a wide variety of programming skills, are a must for this position. The type of programming that machine learning engineers do is very sophisticated. The ability to perform computations and work with complex algorithms is needed in this type of programming.

Strong communication skills are necessary since machine learning engineers will need to explain the process to people who are not programming experts. Some positions also need engineers to publish articles on their work; thus, writing skills are equally important.

UI designer

UI stands for user interface. UI designers are an integral part of the software development team. They are responsible for creating and arranging the visual elements of an application.

User interface is defined as the part of the program that the end-user will see and interact with.

The designers conduct ongoing research on web-based user interface development best practices. They spend most of their time building proof-of-concept mockups, demos, and prototypes for various features. UI designers follow design standards for applications to maintain a consistent look and feel.

Average Salary:

The average salary for a UI designer is $64,740.

Skill Set:

High levels of creativity and professionalism are required. UI design is the most in-demand creative industry right now.

The candidates should possess the ability to be self-directed but also collaborative. They should have amazing communication skills and time-management. Problem-solving skills, along with attention to detail, is required.

UI/UX designers are typically required to have a bachelor's degree in visual design, communications, computer science, or psychology.

If being creative and innovative appeals to you, then UI design is the way to go. Think about the bigger picture, and if designing is your forte, then this role is your ideal choice.

SEO Specialist

SEO stands for Search engine optimization. SEO specialists are responsible for creating and implementing SEO strategies for an organization. Their main job is to ensure that the company appears in the first few pages of search results for relevant keywords. They work with a wide variety of search engines.

SEO specialists tend to focus on one or more types of searches, such as image, video, academic, and local. They continuously stay up to date on new methods for improving their company's online visibility.

Average Salary:

The average salary for a Search Engine Optimization (SEO) Specialist is $45,948.

Skill Set:

Prior experience with SEO is preferred. An SEO specialist should have the ability to understand HTML and CSS. Exposure to various search engines and an in-depth understanding of Google Analytics and Google Webmaster is a bonus. The ability to write web content and design online campaigns for clients is required.

If you are excited about conducting competitive analysis and content optimization, you should begin thinking about this role.

Web Analytics Specialist

Web analytics specialists define metrics, track, analyze, and report on specific project outcomes. They utilize a variety of tools to determine which online marketing strategies are working for a company. They figure out how these efforts can be improved.

These analysts are usually proficient in coding languages and can automate tasks that will be carried out regularly. Analytics is a fast-growing industry with a constant demand for skilled workers. There are endless possibilities for career advancement.

Average Salary:

The average salary for a web analytics specialist is $62,233.

Skill Set:

You should be efficient in importing, cleaning, reviewing, and documenting huge datasets. You'll also need to engage across units to identify and meet data needs. A strong understanding of Google Analytics is necessary for this position. Ability to organize, interpret, and summarize findings by creating reports is preferred.

If you can analyze data using statistical methods to identify trends and meet organizational goals, then web analytics should be your focus.

Enterprise Software Sales

Software sales careers are among the most robust in tech. They usually offer a good degree of job security and huge earning potential at the highest ranks. Enterprise software sales engineers help the client identify needs, match them to the right products, and help close the deal. Whether you have a degree in a technology-related field or experience working for a tech company, you'll be on good footing even if your job wasn't in sales.

Some enterprise software sales positions are account executive, enterprise software account executive, field sales director, sales manager, technical sales engineer, and alliances manager.

Average Salary:

The average enterprise software sales salary is $94,013. The salary range typically falls between $85,900 and $101,846.

Skill Set:

Exceptional skills in sales are needed. Communication skills, along with intensive presentation skills, are preferred.

Growth Hackers

Growth hackers develop new marketing strategies for enhancing an organization's relationship with its customers. They test and execute growth programs on a routine basis. Their main focus is on measuring results by utilizing the latest technology for various organizations and large corporations. Their main goal is to help businesses acquire and retain clients through effective growth programs.

Average Salary:

The average median salary for a growth hacker is $88,609.

Skill Set:

Thinking creatively and implementing innovative ideas is the key to excelling in this role. Excellent technical abilities, strong communication skills, and project management abilities are needed.

Knowledge of Google analytics, search engine optimization, and SQL queries is preferred. Strong collaboration skills are an asset to sustain in a cross-functional team environment.

Do you have amazing project management abilities and can successfully oversee multiple business initiatives and email marketing campaigns? If yes, then a growth hacker is the ideal position for you.

Tech Support Specialist

A technical support specialist offers support to maintain computer hardware and software systems. Their skills are an asset to the company. They are critical to the business as they help resolve technical issues of a customer's accounts or a company's infrastructure. Technical support specialists also support computer software integration by diagnosing and troubleshooting problems.

Average Salary:

Glassdoor suggests the average annual salary for a tech support specialist is $50,000.

Skill Set:

A high school diploma with a bachelor's degree in Computer Science or a related degree is preferred. Some companies require certification in industry-specific networks or operating systems.

Strong customer service background with problem-solving skills are must-have skills. Assisting other team members through help desk software is preferred. Candidates for this role should be open to accepting constructive criticism and customer feedback. Professional written and interpersonal skills are essential.

Technical Recruiter

A technical recruiter is mainly in charge of finding, screening, and selecting talented individuals with technical abilities for various positions as per the company's requirements. They hire candidates from a large pool for tech organizations. Analyzing resumes, work experience, and picking the best fit for the position are the recruiter's main responsibilities. They use their networking abilities to find the best talent in the market.

Average Salary:

Glassdoor suggests the average salary for a technical recruiter is $74,103.

Skill Set:

Good communication skills, hiring skills, and writing skills are needed for this role. Often, establishing and maintaining good relationships with hiring managers is needed to stay on top of current and future hiring needs. You should be able to identify good individuals that fit the organization's work culture.

Game Tester

A game tester's main job is to play while testing the game for glitches and bugs. A quality assurance engineer at a video game company is responsible for developing test cases that check for every possible combination of playing. They aim to break the game. Any code that does not work has to be documented by game testers.

To do this, the engineers are required to be a little unconventional in playing and testing the game at multiple levels. They are responsible for the smooth functioning of the game.

Average Salary:

Glassdoor suggests the average salary for a game QA tester is $55,000.

Skill Set:

A highly detail-oriented candidate is preferred for this job; having laser-focused skills, creativity, and excellent communication is highly necessary.

Do you love playing games? Do you have the ability to think out of the box? If yes, then this role is a perfect match for your skills.

Roja Macherla, Flow manager/Project Manager, USA.

What made you choose the Tech/Engineering field?

Took up Aeronautical Engineering out of so much interest just to realize that I'm a people person and a career in management suits me best. I have an MBA, MS degree under my belt and now my PhD is in progress. In short, I chose a management role in tech industry to fulfill my desire to be in both domains.

What according to you is the main reason for less number of women in the tech/IT industry?

Lack of progressive parental mindset.

What career advice will you give to younger women out there?

Take a breath, understand your strengths and make that passion into a career.

****

Ciprianna Engel, Software Engineer, WP Engine, USA.

What made you choose the Tech/Engineering field?

I began working with data a little in graduate school for a degree in social sciences. I learned that I enjoyed working with data and was lucky to take on a role that allowed me to learn more technical skills when I was out of school. After a while, I decided to commit to learning to code and went through a coding bootcamp focusing on web development. I enjoyed doing that sort of work and was able to get work in software development following the bootcamp.

What according to you is the main reason for less number of women in the tech/IT industry?

I think there are very gendered stereotypes that start at a young age. We hear people continue to encourage boys to learn more technical things. There's this idea that boys like to "tinker" or "break stuff" and put it back together again, but we hardly ever hear that about girls. There is less encouragement for girls to pursue things that are challenging, and that idea is re-enforced throughout school so much that there are very few women in those fields, perpetuating a cycle of perceiving tech as something more suited towards men. At that point, it's difficult for women to break down the barriers because they see less people like them in school and beyond into the workforce.

What career advice will you give to younger women out there?

Do what you love! Trust yourself and ask questions when you need to. Find a mentor that you trust. Be open to new opportunities and be willing to take on things that could lead to something you may have a passion for.

****

Marla Foreman, Software Developer, Fixation Web Consulting, USA.

What made you choose the Tech/Engineering field?

How I ended up in tech/engineering: I loved math and physics in high school. Studied engineering in college, and never left the general engineering/tech area because I never stopped enjoying solving problems. Also, I have a ton of determination. I'm constantly out there climbing some Mount Everest, even when there are a million people saying I'll never make it to the top. Eventually, I do.

How I ended up in my current role: After 10 years in QA, I decided to expand my skills and spent a year and a half teaching myself to code. After that I joined a company to get my foot in the door. I started looking around and somehow fell into my current job, which I am totally loving!

What according to you is the main reason for less number of women in the tech/IT industry?

I'd say the initial introduction to the engineering world probably scares some women off. When I was in college for electrical engineering, we started off with all these hard classes and were thrown right into the deep end. The first couple years were overwhelming. Women can sometimes let their fear get the best of them.

What career advice will you give to younger women out there?

Only do things that you really want to do. It might take some time for exploring and to figure it out, and that's okay.

Don't stick around in a job, a friendship, or a relationship that's very obviously not working out trying to make it work. It's far better to bite the bullet and move on than to waste time. Respect yourself.

Chapter 9

Map Skills to Positions

At this stage, you are aware of your talents, and you also know the different positions available in the computer field. If you are anything like me, one or more of those jobs would have seemed ideal to you and your personality. I would like to think that you have a couple of them picked out already.

You must have thought, "Oh yeah, I can do this. I am good at it," and then you went on to imagine yourself working in that position and delivering 100 percent to the job. You did this by just reading about the job. Imagine what would happen if you had that computer science degree in your arsenal right now. You would better comprehend each of those roles.

The best part is that, unlike me, you now have a clear idea of what you need out of this degree. You have realized what kind of job will suit you the best. For those who do not have any major skills or have not found anything that you excel at yet, I would highly recommend you pick five positions from the list that appeal to you and Google them. Read about those job roles and descriptions.

I also encourage you to attend workshops. Talk to your local Women in Technology chapter, or come find me. Shoot me an email, and we can get going. Hop on to my website to know more about how I can help coach you towards the right field. Don't forget, I told you, I would be the elder sister you never had.

Mapping these skills is important because we tend to be attracted to money in this day and age. Money is tempting, but not always the best answer. The reason I am specifying this step is that I went all in. I became a full-time backend JAVA developer, and I was not happy about it.

I knew that I was a part of a huge project, but somewhere deep down, I knew I lacked motivation. I found a job that helped me satisfy my urge to break the code and be a part of this huge community. I became a developer because it was the highest paying job in the market, yet nobody guided me. However, now I am happy with my salary and my job; I earn enough, and my work brings me joy.

Finding a Career Path:

Where do you find yourself in five years? This is the most awful question in any interview. Well, now, you know. If you could map your skills to a position listed in the previous chapters, you will find yourself looking for a career path in that role.

By career path, I mean the path that will lead you to your ultimate professional goal. Mapping and finding the right role completes 90 percent of the job. You will know what direction you are headed towards in the first six months of your job, and if you do not, you can still switch lanes. Find another professional goal, and walk that path. The most important task will be figuring out if your long-term desire is to be an individual contributor or a leader.

Sample career paths might be:

a) QA Engineer => QA Engineer II => QA Engineer III => QA Lead => QA Manager

or

b) QA Engineer => QA Engineer II => QA Engineer III =>QA Lead => Principal QA Engineer.

So, if someone's goal is to be a manager, then option a is the career path for them, but not everyone wants to manage people. If you don't want to manage people, choose the path of an individual contributor.

One interesting thing to note would be that at this stage, the title will not matter. Your role, job description, and responsibilities will determine your pay package. I have known many Principal QA engineers who earned more money than a QA manager. Salary was determined by career path and experience in the field.

Therefore, spend some time determining what lights you up, and go for it. You are worth it.

Get that computer degree. I promise you it is not super nerdy.

It is fun and lit. You will get a job where you can apply your talent and passion and enjoy your nine to five life.

Stop overwhelming yourself with options. Do your research and map that information to where you are amazing! If you still feel you need more information, utilize online resources, and join crash courses or boot camps.

Find a mentor. Talk to friends and family who are already in the technology sector. Get multiple opinions and ideas. Attend meetups and conferences. Grow your network. Hop on Instagram. Send a DM to a fellow woman in IT, and I promise you, you will not be disappointed at all.

A few of the terms are super technical, but you will realize they are simple when you start learning about them. There is a tool for everything. Some tools in the market sound complicated to use, but when you begin to use certain automation tools, you will see that most of them are drag and drop.

Students in this era are lucky in terms of the abundance of online resources available. Use them to your advantage. Courses, videos, and blogs help you find what you need; go out and get a look and feel of any available technology in the market. Make use of it. Ladies, be smart about where you invest your time.

There is no shame in being a woman in IT. You should be proud of it and smack anyone who thinks otherwise. The IT world needs you and your skill. You need to be the change, and you have got to be in command of your own life.

I want to see each and every girl become independent and manage her own life. Trust me when I tell you that a computer degree is just the beginning of it. It is a whole wide world, and it is changing every minute. Make use of this opportunity and earn vitamin m while you can. You can thank me later. (I love wine btw).

I hope after reading this, you will never offer a blank stare when someone asks you where you see yourself in the next five years.

:) Cheers.

Stephanie Jameson, QA engineer, USA.

What made you choose the Tech/Engineering field?

I wasn't sure what to do with my math degree right out of college, and a friend suggested applying for a job at a QA consulting company. Applied through LinkedIn easy apply, and then went very quickly through the interview process.

What according to you is the main reason for less number of women in the tech/IT industry?

Less awareness of the job opportunities, and less awareness of how cool it is and pushing in that direction at younger ages. It still isn't considered "cool" for girls.

What career advice will you give to younger women out there?

Don't let others push you around because you are a woman. Stand confident in your knowledge. Don't let men make you second guess what you know.

****

Bhavya Mukkera, Solutions Engineer, Phenom People, India.

What made you choose the Tech/Engineering field?

I was a below avg student in academics. I never wanted to study. Engineering was never my choice; it was my father's desire. I pushed myself hard to graduate. All my friends started getting offers in multinational companies. I was selected for a company out of 300 students, but since the office was in a different location, my parents asked me to decline the offer.

I finally landed a job as a Business development associate for a startup. I slowly advanced in the same role but switched to different IT organizations.

What according to you is the main reason for less number of women in the tech/IT industry?

Most people think that it is all about coding and that women can't do it. They presume that it is tough to be in the IT field.

What career advice will you give to younger women out there?

IT is not about coding. There are a lot of opportunities out there. Explore! Talk to people, have meaningful conversations, analyze what makes you happy. Be passionate about what you are doing. Also, don't stop learning.

Chapter 10

My Story

By now, I have mentioned many times that I was born in India, a still developing country. My mother did not know better, so she asked me to join engineering, and my life changed after the year 2009.

I was at the top of my university class all four years, and my name is now on the board of my college. I take pride in that. I was the first person to get hired through the on-campus placements, and I was on top of the world.

I thought I would never have to worry. India is a very big country with a *lot* of people. So, competition is everywhere. Getting a job during your final year meant that you were set for the next five years and had nothing to worry about.

After graduation, I waited for seven months, but I never received a formal joining date from the company that hired me. By this time, a few of my friends who had lesser packages had already begun earning. The rest were busy packing to move abroad for higher education.

My mother clearly told me that America would not be possible because we did not have an asset to get a student loan. I was not surprised, and I was not disheartened because I had a good-paying job offer—without a joining date.

After some time, my mother got a promotion and asked me to apply to universities. She thought she could now arrange my tuition. I nodded my head as usual—it is in every Indian's blood to nod at everything.

I passed my GRE and aced the IELTS test. I began applying to universities. I got a letter of acceptance from three universities. I wanted to go to the Illinois Institute of Technology Chicago, but the I20 had an amount that I had never dreamt of.

The University of Nebraska Omaha, on the other hand, offered me a scholarship, and obviously, I had to choose that. I studied hard for two years, and in the summer of 2015, I bagged an internship as a developer at a Fortune 500 company in Omaha. That, my friends, was the turning point for me.

My team was amazing, and everyone helped me all the time, but job satisfaction was zilch. I told my manager that I saw myself as a Business Analyst or a QA Engineer, and he told me that though that sounded wonderful, he would only be able to extend a full-time offer if I joined as a developer.

I am glad I did not follow the crowd, and I determined my own path. One that in which I'd find joy working eight hours a day for the next five years.

I was interviewed by super cool people at my previous organization, a startup, and the manager there asked me this burning question. He asked, "Your resume and work experience are all about JAVA, and you were a software engineer, so why QA?"

I told him I love to break the code more than writing it, and he immediately offered me the position of QA Engineer.

Since then, I have spoken at multiple international tech conferences. I found a role that satisfied my love for tech, my nature of finding weird stuff, my appreciation for attention to detail, and my love for presentations.

All this was possible because I declined to be in a role that I was not suited for.

I found other opportunities and later moved to another startup in Omaha. This time I got a role that was all about data testing. I didn't know anything about ETL, but I learned about it. Thanks to my current company mentor, I love ETL, and I love data now.

I found a tool to automate manual testing with millions of records in the database. One day as I was working with this automation tool, I realized that not everyone knows about such tools. I did not know what ETL automation was until I joined this company and the best part was that it did not involve coding. We needed a solution that would be easy for others to learn and start implementing.

This was how I began to think about the young women out there who have no clue about the computer industry. They think it is hard, but it is not once one learns and implements the concepts.

Diversity is lacking in the tech industry. Only a handful of women work in IT, and even those in it have no clue of the variety of tools that are available in the market. Many tools provide different solutions, and most importantly, not all require programming.

I figured that if I could learn all this and teach an entire team without prior coding experience to use this tool, then I could do that for anyone who knows about computers and is willing to learn. I realized that I could make anyone the "IT Girl."

I went back to the basics. I wanted to teach women about different tools in tech. However, I thought, "What if there aren't enough women to teach?" In my research for this book, I learned about the prevailing stigma in society about women in tech.

If you are willing to learn, then nothing is difficult. If you are eager and want to make something out of your career, then you must get into tech.

My sister had no interest in information technology. She wanted to be a fashion designer. She took a gap year then prepared for a university exam. She secured a decent rank and got a seat at the National Institute of Fashion Technology in a remote part of India.

My mother immediately intervened and was not ready to send my sister away for a degree in fashion. My sister was forced to study for the engineering entrance exam and step into tech for four years. She is now a project manager for a firm in Hyderabad, India.

She did not choose to be a developer, either. She knew that being able to design processes would be her forte, so she steered her career towards success. She earns well, loves her job, and is happy today.

I personally get inspired by real-life stories, and so I added testimonials from real women in the tech world. Everyone has been confused at one point or the other in terms of career. This is a small attempt from me to help remove any confusion for you.

I will be the happiest person on earth if at least one person finds this book inspiring and helpful.

I had nobody to guide me, and I know the pain of getting what you want in life by trial and error. So, I don't want you or your daughter/sister/friend/relative/partner to make the same mistake.

If I can come from a third world country, without any guidance and design a path for myself, then you can do it too.

It does not matter in which part of the world you live if your passion drives you and keeps you up at night.

It doesn't matter if you are rich or poor. If you have the liberty to select a major for yourself, then make the right choice because whatever you choose will determine your present and future.

Get strong, sound smart, and be good at whatever you do; give it your all. Look around you and get inspired. Have a healthy competition with yourself, and most of all, check-in with yourself occasionally to ensure you are still happy and sane.

Join tech and see the difference for yourself. Get lit in tech.

Don't just get addicted to technology. Be obsessed with it.

Will you be the next *IT Girl*?

References:

"Women in Tech: The Facts (2016 Update)," May 13,2016. https://www.ncwit.org/resources/women-tech-facts-2016-update.

"NCWIT Fact Sheet." National Center for Women & Information Technology. Accessed January 3, 2021. https://www.ncwit.org/ncwit-fact-sheet.

White, Sarah K. "Women in Tech Statistics: The Hard Truths of an Uphill Battle." CIO. CIO, January 23, 2020. https://www.cio.com/article/3516012/women-in-tech-statistics-the-hard-truths-of-an-uphill-battle.html.

"Computer Science." Encyclopædia Britannica. Encyclopædia Britannica, inc. Accessed January 3, 2021. https://www.britannica.com/science/computer-science.

"15-1211 Computer Systems Analysts." U.S. Bureau of Labor Statistics. U.S. Bureau of Labor Statistics, July 6, 2020. https://www.bls.gov/oes/current/oes151211.htm.

"Average Project Manager, Information Technology (IT) Salary." PayScale. Accessed January 3, 2021. https://www.payscale.com/research/US/Job=Project_Manager,_Information_Technology_(IT)/Salary.

"Women in the Labor Force: a Databook : BLS Reports." U.S. Bureau of Labor Statistics. U.S. Bureau of Labor Statistics, December 1, 2019.

https://www.bls.gov/opub/reports/womens-databook/2019/home.htm.

"Computer and Information Technology Occupations : Occupational Outlook Handbook." U.S. Bureau of Labor Statistics. U.S. Bureau of Labor Statistics, September 1, 2020. https://www.bls.gov/ooh/computer-and-information-technology/.

Robert Half. "Want to Become a Systems Engineer? Here Are the Skills Required." Systems Engineer Job and Salary | Robert Half. Robert Half, October 17, 2019. https://www.roberthalf.com/blog/salaries-and-skills/want-to-become-a-systems-engineer-here-are-the-skills-required.

"Sales Engineers : Occupational Outlook Handbook." U.S. Bureau of Labor Statistics. U.S. Bureau of Labor Statistics, September 1, 2020. https://www.bls.gov/ooh/sales/sales-engineers.htm.

"Management Analysts : Occupational Outlook Handbook." U.S. Bureau of Labor Statistics. U.S. Bureau of Labor Statistics, September 1, 2020. https://www.bls.gov/ooh/business-and-financial/management-analysts.htm.

"Computer and Information Technology Occupations : Occupational Outlook Handbook." U.S. Bureau of Labor Statistics. U.S. Bureau of Labor Statistics, September 1, 2020. https://www.bls.gov/ooh/computer-and-information-technology/home.htm.

Asare, Janice Gassam. "The 25 Highest-Paying Jobs In America In 2018." Forbes. Forbes Magazine, August 15, 2018.

https://www.forbes.com/sites/janicegassam/2018/08/15/the-25-highest-paying-jobs-in-america-in-2018/?sh=4bc5d5595fd5.

Tech Support Specialist Salaries. Glassdoor, December 16, 2020. https://www.glassdoor.com/Salaries/tech-support-specialist-salary-SRCH_KO0,23.htm?clickSource=searchBtn.

Game Tester Salaries. Glassdoor, December 12, 2020. https://www.glassdoor.com/Salaries/game-tester-salary-SRCH_KO0,11.htm?clickSource=searchBtn

"2019 Scrum Master Trends- An Update to Age of Product's 2017 Scrum Master Salary Report Following the Profession's Most Comprehensive Survey Ever Conducted." Scrum, 2019. https://scrumorg-website-prod.s3.amazonaws.com/drupal/2019-02/2019%20Scrum%20Master%20Trends%20%282019-02-06%29.pdf.

"How Much Is a Data Scientist's Salary?: University of Wisconsin." University of Wisconsin Data Science Degree, September 25, 2020. https://datasciencedegree.wisconsin.edu/data-science/data-scientist-salary/.

"Graphic Designers: Occupational Outlook Handbook." U.S. Bureau of Labor Statistics. U.S. Bureau of Labor Statistics, September 1, 2020. https://www.bls.gov/ooh/arts-and-design/graphic-designers.htm.

"Average Development Operations (DevOps) Engineer Salary." PayScale. Accessed January 3, 2021.

https://www.payscale.com/research/US/Job=Development_O
perations_(DevOps)_Engineer/Salary.

Kapin, Allyson. "10 Stats That Build The Case For Investing In
Women-Led Startups." Forbes. Forbes Magazine, January 28,
2019.
https://www.forbes.com/sites/allysonkapin/2019/01/28/10-
stats-that-build-the-case-for-investing-in-women-led-
startups/?sh=32a7565159d5.

Wong, Julia Carrie. "Women Considered Better Coders – but
Only If They Hide Their Gender." The Guardian. Guardian News
and Media, February 12, 2016.
https://www.theguardian.com/technology/2016/feb/12/wo
men-considered-better-coders-hide-gender-github.

Acknowledgments:

Thank you to everyone who submitted your own experience and for reaching out. This book would not have been possible without all you Rockstar women in Technology.

Author Bio

Sheekha Singh grew up in Hyderabad, India, worked in the U.S.A for seven years, and currently lives in Kitchener, Canada.

She loves writing, traveling, reading, and drinking coffee and wine. She has a bachelor's degree in Computer Science from JNTU (India) and ranked first in her university. She has a Master's degree in Management Information Systems from the University of Nebraska, Omaha. (U.S.A). Sheekha currently works as a QA Engineer. She was listed in the Agile Testing Days' list of 125 awesome testers to keep an eye on the year 2017.

Sheekha has been a speaker at various international tech conferences and is the founder of a non-profit in India. She has been the recipient of many awards from childhood. She is passionate about many things; helping young women and encouraging them to build strong careers has been her keen area of interest. She also blogs and maintains a writer profile on Instagram under the handle @sheekhasingh_writer.

She loves planning trips and visiting new places. When Sheekha is not working, she is either reading or planning her next trip.

Fun Fact: She technically drowned in the Atlantic Ocean for a minute.

Review Ask

Love this book? Don't forget to leave a review!

Every review matters, and it matters a *lot to me!*

Head over to Amazon or wherever you purchased this book to leave an honest review for me.

I thank you endlessly.

Also, do not forget to post a picture on social media with hashtag #theitgirl and tag me in your pictures.

Made in the USA
Middletown, DE
19 March 2023

27115630R00076